Dealing with Difficult Metamours

DEALING WITH DIFFICULT METAMOURS

PAGE TURNER

Braided Studios, LLC
PO Box 770670
Lakewood, OH 44107
https://braided.studio

Published By: Braided Studios, LLC

ISBN: 978-1-947296-04-6

A special thanks to our Patreons

Elan

Tom

Dave

Jacinta

Jason

Jennifer

Kaizen

Kit

Lee

Nada

Rain

William

Allyson	Jenny
Anna	Jo
Beverly	Libby
Brendan	Llew
Endre	Maureen
Gregg	Pour
Jason	Reino
Jeffery	Stephanie

Contents

Introduction

General Principles

Metamour Types

Other Scenarios

Tools & Exercises

Appendix

Metamour

noun.

A romantic partner's other partner

Polyamory

noun.

The practice of participating simultaneously in more than one serious romantic or sexual relationship with the knowledge and consent of all partners

Section 1
Introduction

Introduction

In a lot of the polyamory how-to, we're very partner centered. Even questions like "how do I manage jealousy?" tend to have our partner at the center of it, as something that is gained or lost and the metamour (i.e., your partner's other partner) simply a happenstance agent of that scary change.

But it's not our partners that really make the daily existence of polyamory that different from monogamy. Sure, you're busier, and you may have layers of feelings that you've never dealt with, but honestly where polymory and monogamy really seem to diverge is because of metamours. The fact that you have these people in your life who love the same people you love.

Metamour relations are a form of improv — sometimes hilarious, sometimes awkward, sometimes painful, sometimes glorious. But never dull.

It can be tricky navigating these friendships (and lots of them, if you're well connected) that there simply is no script for.

Or is there?

Here's the kicker – we actually had plenty of good models around us. They just weren't romantic.

You ever know someone who had two best friends? I sure have.

Being metamours with someone can be an awful lot like sharing a best friend. Sometimes you'll run into cross-purposes when trying to make plans with your best friend. They'll have made plans to go off and do something else with their other friend.

Sometimes, you're welcome to come along, too. But sometimes it isn't something that can work out that way.

Just like a co-best friend, sometimes your metamour will become *your* best friend, too. But sometimes? It's a regular friendship.

And in some cases, for whatever reason, you really don't get along with them.

That's where this book comes in.

While I've tried my best in this book whenever possible to provide practical solutions and actionable steps, when it comes to other people, there is almost never any one quick and easy method.

As much as it might be easier, we can't control other people. Nor should we. Sometimes if we're lucky, we can *influence* them. But the final decision of how people want to act is nearly always up to them.

You'll notice that this book is not called *Fixing Difficult Metamours*. That's because it's not up to us to fix other people and not really something we can or should be doing. What we can do, however, is learn how to best deal with them.

Because while we don't control how other people act, with practice and sustained attention, we can learn to control how *we* act and how we *choose to respond* to the actions of others.

This can involve:

1. Changing the way that we interact with them

2. Changing how we perceive them and their actions

3. Learning better ways to cope with what will always bother us

Or any mixture of the three.

What approach is appropriate will depend on the given situation you find yourself in, but my goal in this book is to give you plenty of tools to do these things.

While there's plenty to be learned from tackling this book on your own, you're likely to find the most benefit if you read this with your metamour and shared partner.

If you're reading this book along with your metamour and partner, please see "A Readers' Discussion Guide for Vees" on page 157 for questions you can all answer as you read through it that can help facilitate discussions.

Look in the Mirror First

If one person calls you an ass, ignore him. If two men call you an ass, start looking for tracks. If three men call you an ass, put on a harness.

-Proverb

If you run into an asshole in the morning, you ran into an asshole. If you run into assholes all day, you're the asshole.

-Elmore Leonard

Knowing your own darkness is the best method for dealing with the darknesses of other people.

-Carl Jung

As you go through this book, parts of it are likely to resonate with you. And not just as things that *other people* do. But maybe even things that you yourself do or have done in the past.

The truth is that all of us are capable of being someone else's difficult metamour. Everybody's someone else's difficult person at least some of the time.

Part of being compassionate when other people are engaging in difficult behaviors (which helps us be more patient with them) involves keeping this in mind: That sometimes the difficult person is you.

Meeting Your Metamours (or Not)

The role metamours play (or don't play) in your life can vary dramatically depending on how much time you spend with them.

Some people live with all of their metamours and partners like one big happy family, while others never even meet the other people their partners are dating.

Here are two common terms that people use to discuss varying levels of metamour contact.

Kitchen Table Polyamory – a style of polyamory where everyone in the polyamorous relationship system is comfortable sitting down at the kitchen table with one another to have a cup of coffee (or hot chocolate, soda, whatever is your speed)

Parallel Polyamory – a style of polyamory where relationships run in parallel and metamours don't meet or interact with one another

While in my poly circles I do know a few people who employ a more parallel style of polyamory, I generally tend to be very kitchen table in my own approach. This is because I would find it fiendishly difficult to have an ongoing romantic relationship with someone who would not meet my other partners, especially if they refused to meet my nesting partner. Logistically speaking alone, it would be a total nightmare. I live with my nesting partner. I hang out with him a lot. Scheduling around that would be annoyingly difficult.

The other big issue is that anybody who wouldn't want to meet my nesting partner probably wouldn't be all that keen on my talking about him. And as expected, I talk about him. A lot. He's a big part of my life. We do a lot of things together. He's my best friend. He's important to me. He is an extremely significant other. Tact is one thing, being gentle about other connections but never mentioning him? Pretending he doesn't exist? It would be an exhausting mental exercise to censor, redirect, find other ways to discuss whatever issue involves him or is somehow connected to him.

So that's one con about keeping things separate. It's a lot of work to self-censor and compartmentalize.

And there's the additional issue that even if you can keep things completely separate in the short term that there may times when unintentional overlaps happen.

I've worked with clients with a parallel poly setup who stumbled into situations where due to wild coincidences of social media and general "small world" randomness that they crossed paths anyway. For example, a good friend of mine reevaluated their practice of avoiding each other's partners when her husband's girlfriend ran into them at the movies.

While the initial introduction can be awkward, especially if one or both of you is newer to polyamory, it can be really help to meet your metamour at least once. Here are just a few benefits:

- It helps you to know the person your partner is spending so much time with as an actual person, not as a shadowy imaginary being. This can give you a valuable frame of reference when your partner is talking about their interactions with your metamour. People often report experiencing decreased jealousy once they've put a face to the name. As one client I spoke with put it: "Everyone's a billionaire supermodel in my head. I'm a wreck until I meet new metamours. Seeing an actual person with just as many strengths and flaws as I have totally helps put those feelings to bed."

- Meeting your metamour helps to ensure that everyone is aware of one another and is a way to confirm that everyone is somewhat comfortable with the polyamorous nature of the relationships. Sadly, there have been incidents of people claiming to be polyamorous with their other partner's support who are actually cheating on that partner. Meeting your partner's other partner helps to eliminate this possibility.

- Knowing your metamour can help tremendously with logistics. In the event that schedules need to be cross-referenced quickly, it can sometimes be more expedient for metamours to work directly with one another rather than all communications being filtered through their mutual partner.

- It enables you to scheme against your mutual partner. Bhahaha. Only half-joking on this one. Because seriously, two heads are better than one when planning a kickass surprise party or coordinating what gifts to get your mutual partner for their birthday.

Now, meeting your metamour doesn't mean that you're going to be expected to date them as well (and anyone who pressures you to is being icky).

Nor does it even mean that you're going to end up being friends with them (although it's really great and convenient when a metamour ends up being a friend).

It's just an introduction and an acknowledgement of one another. Nothing more, nothing less.

O

Sometimes meeting your metamour in person isn't terribly practical. You might work opposite schedules Or perhaps your partner is in a long-distance relationship and travels to see your metamour while you stay at home.

In cases like these, technology is your friend. Even a virtual meeting (via email, IM, or video chat) can serve to break a lot of the tension and make things more comfortable.

What If My Metamour Doesn't Want to Meet Me?

A metamour who doesn't want to meet you is a definite sign for caution as it could be a sign of larger problems.

It could mean that your partner and metamour haven't really handled the insecurities that can sprout from dating others. And while this may just be a temporary state, left unchecked, this can wreak havoc on every relationship involved – your relationship with your partner, your partner's relationship with your metamour, and any that your metamour may be having with others.

Working past the insecurities that come with adjusting to consensual nonmonogamy can be difficult work that many couples avoid. But it's necessary.

Additionally, as mentioned above, the other common risk that comes from not meeting your metamour is that they might be engaging in infidelity.

Proceeding without meeting your metamour (at least virtually) puts you at risk. This is not to say that you can't accept that level of risk and continue with your relationship without meeting your metamour. But it's definitely something to be conscious about and to consider.

Triangular Communication: Another Potential Pitfall of Not Meeting Your Metamour

"Tell your girlfriend that…"

"Would you ask so-and-so if they can…"

We're likely all guilty of doing this now and again, conveying a message to someone else via a third party.

When done in moderation, some forms of triangular communication can be harmless. For example: Do I really need to directly invite someone to a party, when I've sent the invitation via their live-in partner and explained they are both welcome? Probably not (although depending on the exact circumstances, this simple act might make that other person feel slighted or unimportant).

But in other instances, triangular communication can devolve into a manipulative tactic where parties are being played against one another.

At the very least, just like a childhood game of Telephone, conveying messages through an intermediary can promote to misunderstanding and a lack of clarity.

Whenever possible, it's best to be able to address issues directly with the person that you're having them with.

Unfortunately, if you never meet your metamour, any communication you have with them is likely to be triangular in nature, leading to a higher risk of being misunderstood and opening up the door for the onset of manipulative communication patterns, even if nobody has this intention setting out.

Section 2

-

General Principles

Identify What's Bothering You and Why

While far from an exhaustive listing of all the ways that metamours can be troubling, this book outlines some of the common ones and can help you zero in on solutions.

Please see the individual subsections on problem metamour types for help identifying them.

But not all of it can come from a book. The other half comes from you.

The first thing you need to do is ask yourself: "Why don't I like this person?" or if you like them well enough but are still experiencing stress, "What is really bothering me about them?

It could just be a personality conflict (which totally happens, not everyone is going to be best friends). But here are some questions that can help you narrow things down and see if it's another common reason:

Do I feel like they're smarter, funnier, prettier, sexier, or somehow "better" than me?

If so, it's time to invest that worried energy into dealing with those insecurities. If this is the main reason you object to the relationship, it's likely to happen again with someone else your partner dates. It's better just to take care of the root problem (please see "Five Steps to Feeling Safe and Secure in Polyamory" on page 149).

Do they remind me of someone from my past that I don't like?

Sometimes we meet someone, and for no clear reason, we dislike them instantly. Or we're incredibly jealous of them. Sometimes it's both. We do not come into relationships unbiased. Instead, we enter them as a collection of all of our life experiences. Transference happens when we unconsciously direct feelings we have for a person we've known in the past onto a new person. While this transference effect is powerful and can feel real, it's more often misleading and typically does not provide helpful information or signals that we should trust.

Do I feel like this partner is too different from me? And that it means that my partner doesn't really want someone like me?

This happens most often in people who are new to non-monogamy. They'll take their partner's taste in other people very personally. I walked right into this trap myself when I was newly polyamorous. I looked at my partner's partner selections as a referendum on me as a person. To the brain weasels of my anxiety, every time my partner chose someone to date, he was giving me secret messages about how he viewed me. The things he wanted to tell me but couldn't bear to be honest enough to say. So when someone he dated was very different from me and/or someone different than who *I* would have chosen, I would get upset.

What worked for me to break out of these patterns was remembering my confusion as a teenager when my mother would get upset and say, "Do you know how what you've done makes *me* look?"

While she was (perhaps rightfully, perhaps not) worried about how others in the community would judge her parenting abilities, this remark made little sense to me because I knew I was my own person and making decisions based on my values. And not hers.

It took a bit of doing, but as I adjusted to polyamory, I came to realize that my partner, too, was their own person and that their partner selections aren't a referendum on me as a person.

Do they have a reputation for treating others badly?

This is something that might be worth paying a lot of attention to. Now, bear in mind that what people say about others is subjective. Consider the source of the information (for example, we have a person in our local community who bad mouths *everyone* like the Boy Who Cried Wolf). Just because one person has a bad experience with someone, it doesn't mean that others will.

However, routinely difficult people often have a traceable trail of bad run-ins with others, so I pay extra attention to people who have established a pattern of doing things I find unacceptable (e.g., abuse, extremely controlling behavior, violating consent, etc). Because while people can change over time, it isn't guaranteed to happen.

Did they treat my partner badly in the past?

Hands down, this is my Achilles' heel. When one of my partners decides they want to re-date an ex who wasn't great to them, I struggle. And struggle. My brain boils.

Are they treating my partner badly now or doing something else that's causing problems?

This is also my Achilles' heel. I apparently have two Achilles' heels.

The guy likely had two feet, so why not, right? Who's to say Achilles wasn't held by both feet when they dunked him in the River Styx? There weren't photographers then.

The first three reasons (feeling someone's better than you, reminds you of someone from your past you don't like, or isn't the person *you* would choose for your partner) can be very uncomfortable but bear little cause for practical concern. They are best addressed with self-work.

This *can* involve speaking through things with your partner or metamour, but ultimately the responsibility falls on you to reframe and rethink the underlying beliefs. Please see "Five Steps to Feeling Safe and Secure in Polyamory" on page 149 for help on how to do that.

With the next two reasons (a reputation for treating others badly or a history of being bad to your partner) you may just be on to something. But even so, be careful to check your biases and make sure that there isn't some of the bias from #1, 2, and/or 3 mixed in with your concerns.

And if it's the final reason, you are reading the right book.

Things to keep in mind:

- While behavior can be frustrating, people *aren't* their behavior. You can still recognize someone's humanity and other good qualities even if they do things that really get your goat.

- Behavior falls into patterns. This can be trying, as you may deal with the same problems over and over. However, on the other hand, the fact that problems repeat mean that you can learn to identify, anticipate, and react to those behaviors in ways that work better.

Try to Understand Them

"Do unto others twenty-five percent better than you expect them to do unto you...The twenty-five percent is for error."

-Linus Pauling

Perspective-taking can go a long way in bridging the gap between you and a difficult metamour.

Taking someone else's perspective isn't always easy. We tend to get locked into our emotions and look at the world through our particular filter. It can be easy to forget that other people view things differently, and by forgetting that, misunderstandings often result.

But what if we could break that pattern? What if we could respond to difficult conflicts not with frustration but with empathy for the other person's situation?

Empathy Exercises

There are four main ways to build empathy:

1. Make Opportunities to Listen

2. Reverse Engineer

3. The Shape-Shifting Game

4. Meditation and Visualization

Make Opportunities to Listen

"We have two ears and one mouth, so we should listen more than we say."

-Zeno of Citium

*

"When people talk, listen completely. Most people never listen."

-Ernest Hemingway

In conversation, far too many of us are focused not on listening to what others are saying but on formulating what we're going to say in response.

Pay attention to how you communicate with others. Experiment with asking someone new once a day how they're doing. If they respond with one of those automatic answers like "fine" or "okay," ask again: "No, I really want to know. How are you?"

Now if they give that pat answer again, then don't push any further. Sometimes people aren't in the mood to discuss how things are going.

But be available and open. Practice empathetic listening (also known as relationship listening).

It's a difficult style that can be exhausting to do correctly. It takes a lot of attention and emotional labor.

In the empathetic style, we actively listen, not with the goal of responding or applying the information to practical purpose, but to *understand* the speaker so that we can help them emotionally.

The core skill of this style of active listening is quite simple: Restating what the other person has said to you, indicating that you understand. And this restatement should be a paraphrase or summary. With no judgement, no advice. Just giving them a simple sign that their message got across and you understand. And asking for confirmation if you're unsure.

"So what I'm hearing is that you're frustrated with your work load."

"It sounds like you'd like more dates with me on weekends and not just weeknights. Is that correct?"

Here are some things to avoid while actively listening:

- Interrupting. Cues that people are done speaking can be unclear, so if you do interrupt, apologize and allow them to speak.

- Asking "why?" questions. These often make people defensive.

- Giving unsolicited advice. If you have something you'd like to give input on, bridge the gap by asking for their consent. "Could I make a suggestion?" (And be okay if with a "no" if they refuse.)

- Reassuring them too quickly. "Don't worry, you'll be fine" is usually said in a well-meaning way but will often come off as dismissive.

- Using the time that they're speaking to formulate your own response. You can do that after they are done speaking.

Reverse Engineer

Think of a puzzling interaction you had with someone else you didn't understand. Sit down and think of reasons why the person could have acted that way. List as many as you possibly can. When writing down all of the reasons, don't just focus on ones that paint them in a negative light. Think of as many contingencies that could have come up that could have been responsible.

When doing this, it may help to think of times in your own life when you've acted similarly and what was going on at the time.

The Shape-Shifting Game

Go to a public place and observe people discreetly. Pretend you are them. What are you thinking? What was your morning like? Daydream about their possible inner lives. Make up back stories. Have fun with this one.

It doesn't matter if you're right or wrong in these invented histories. What's important is that you're deeply imagining what it might be like to be someone else.

Metta-mours: The Loving Kindness Meditation

This last exercise comes from Buddhism, where it's known as metta practice. The word *metta* comes from Pali and roughly means "loving-kindness."

To do this meditation, offer loving wishes to yourself and others with each breath you take. There are several different ways to word it, but here's one I've found personally helpful:

May I be happy,

May I be free,

May I awaken to the light of my true nature,

May I be loved.

*

Start with yourself, then move the loving thoughts to someone close to you – a friend or family member.

May [Friend] be happy,

May [Friend] be free,

May [Friend] awaken to the light of their true nature,

May [Friend] be loved.

*

After directing these thoughts to a friend or family member, direct them towards an acquaintance or someone you barely know.

Once you've done that, direct those feelings towards someone you struggle with – a difficult person, perhaps even an enemy.

Take your time as you direct these thoughts. Do them slowly with your breath. Don't rush through the thoughts or fake the positivity.

Repeat them until you start to feel them take hold.

As you get used to these exercises, you'll find patterns that work best for you, as far as order (even perhaps directing positive wishes to the whole world or a lover, once you get the hang of things). But always start with yourself. And if you need to work on self-compassion, you might want to end with yourself as well.

Polyamory and Boundaries

One of the trickiest parts of polyamory is determining whether or not something you're doing affects someone else.

In a more simple relationship system, like monogamy, this is a great deal more straightforward. You have one person's concerns to consider. When you start considering how decisions could impact metamours and telemours (your meta's metamour), and how all of their decisions potentially affect you? Well, things get a great deal more complicated.

They weren't just being cute with that "it's complicated" relationship status. Polyamory gets interesting. But first, the basics of boundary setting!

Boundary Setting 101

Asserting boundaries is about establishing what you are or are not okay with.

Boundaries are particularly important in achieving healthy relationships with others.

Boundaries are *very* individual. They call them *personal* boundaries for a reason.

But as a starting point here are some basic healthy boundaries to keep in mind:

- Not allowing others to manipulate or force you into doing things you don't want to do. And not doing so to anyone else.

- Not tolerating others yelling at you or calling you names. And not doing this to others.

- Not blaming others for things that are your responsibility. And not tolerating inappropriate blaming from others.

- Understanding that your feelings are separate from another person's, although you certainly can have empathy for their situation.

- Being able to request space (physical, temporal, privacy, etc) and allowing others to request the same from you.

To a lot of recovering people pleasers, setting these boundaries can seem daunting. Even controlling. But boundary setting is different from controlling people, which is about telling other people what to do. Especially when it has little or nothing to do with you.

Here are some simple boundary-setting statements:

- "I'm not willing to argue with you right now. I'd be happy to talk to you later when we're both calm."

- "I'm sorry, but I won't be doing that. I won't be loaning you any more money until you pay off what I loaned you before."

Whenever possible, use as non-blaming language as possible. Be firm, but not on the attack. Generally speaking, "I" statements come off as more diplomatic than "you" statements.

So rather than saying, "You're always snooping through my stuff," try saying:

"I feel violated when you look through my things. I need some privacy in a relationship. Otherwise, I feel like I'm under a magnifying glass. Please do not go through my things without asking."

Bear in mind that it's possible to use "I" statements in an aggressive or ineffective way. "I feel that you're always snooping through my stuff," or "I hate that you're always snooping through my stuff," are both blaming and ineffective.

While you *might* feel that blame is warranted, blaming others put them on the defensive, which makes them less likely to listen and accommodate your needs. Avoid blanket generalized statements including words like "always" and "never." These feel particularly unfair to a person receiving them. It's a rare person who does something always or never. And the exaggeration aspect undercuts the truth of what you're saying.

Instead, focus on your feelings.

When setting boundaries, it can be helpful to share the potential consequences of violating that boundary. However, be honest with yourself and your partners as you do. Don't threaten things you aren't willing to follow through on. If you say you'll have to leave a relationship over a certain behavior, be prepared to do so. Conserve these consequences for the worst violations. And especially after repeated violations with no efforts to improve.

Thankfully, proposed consequences need not be so dire. Using the last example about snooping, you might tell your partner that if they don't stop looking through your things, you will have to lock your things up. Or change your passwords on a computer.

If you find that the issue of invasion of your privacy is widespread and particularly troubling, causing you to feel disrespected in a way that harms your relationship, you might pursue counseling. Or, as mentioned, there is always ending the relationship (just don't start there if you can help it).

If at all possible, it's best to discuss what your boundaries are *before* they're violated. I'm aware of most of mine due to past life experiences I've had. I find it goes more smoothly if you can preemptively share those with new partners. Not only are new partners less likely to violate those boundaries, but if they do? The resulting discussion usually entails less conflict and drama if it's not completely new information to them.

Second-Degree Boundaries and Beyond

Okay, now that we have a basic intro to boundaries, we're all set to tackle polyamory with them, right?

Hold on there.

We have officially arrived at the tricky part.

Traditional boundary-setting tackles first-degree boundaries, that is, your direct interactions with another person.

What about second-degree boundaries? Your metamour's interactions with your partner? It's easy when they don't affect you at all. But what if they do? How about beyond the second degree — your telemour (your meta's partner)?

What's particularly difficult about polyamory is not only figuring out how to set boundaries that keep you emotionally healthy. It's doing that in a multi-person system where things still affect you. But without meddling in stuff that has little or nothing to do with you. Many people seek out polyamory as a relationship style *because* they connect easily with others.

And while this can be great, poor boundaries aren't just about letting people walk all over you. They can also involve succumbing to your Inner Buttinski.

Three Buckets of Control to Sort Them All!

An important distinction to make is between things you can control, things you can kind of control, and things you can't control at all.

Let's think of this as three buckets.

In the first bucket are the decisions you consciously make. Simple stuff like what you choose to wear in the morning. And more complicated stuff like how you talk to your partners. Maybe you can't always control your initial emotional reaction to something, but you can control the actions that you take based on that emotion.

The second bucket is the influence bucket. Let's say a friend or loved one asks for your advice about something. You can tell them what you think, but they still make the decision what they're going to do with your input.

The third bucket is stuff you can't control. Weather. Traffic. The actions of strangers or of people who don't care at all what you think.

Boundaries and the Buckets of Control

First-degree boundaries are set in the first bucket. You choose to tell the other person what you want or need to happen. And you control the way that you deliver that message.

When it comes to whether or not people abide by the boundaries that you set, that's the second bucket. You've influenced them by sharing your viewpoint, but they control how they respond to that.

However, if they violate that boundary or do not accept it as legitimate, you are back in the first bucket. You control what you say or do next. What consequences or possible solutions you offer.

The tricky part of second-degree boundaries is that you may very well see behavior from your metamour towards your love that you would never, *ever* tolerate were it done to you. Maybe your meta continually cancels dates with your love without notice. It's hurtful and inconvenient for them.

Can you set a personal boundary with your metamour as a second-degree one? "I will no longer allow you to see my partner if you keep canceling on them last minute."

Well, you *can* do this. But you really shouldn't. Buttinski Sign! That's not your relationship.

It's understandable that you're frustrated. When you love someone, you feel empathy for things that hurt them, but if it doesn't directly impact you in a logistical way just be there for your partner. If they want your input and you feel comfortable giving it, help them figure out how to address this with your metamour. But otherwise, chill.

Now, if the frequent cancellations are impacting your plans and you find that you're inconvenienced by multiple reschedules that your partner has to make with the flaky metamour, then it's entirely appropriate to set a personal boundary with your partner surrounding the rescheduling. It's entirely inappropriate to *expect* you to accommodate for someone else who is not keeping their commitments. If you *want* to, fine. But you may find you want or need to set a boundary around it. But with your *partner*. Not your metamour.

That's the key, really. Whenever an issue further on in the relationship system (web, polycule, poly family, etc) is impacting you, look at what personally affects you. And when looking to negotiate those agreements, work first with those who are in your immediate sphere.

Don't run from conflicts that you need to address. But don't go rustling through the bushes looking for something to fight.

Good Partner Selection is Key

I get a lot of different questions from people who know I'm polyamorous and think it would be a difficult way to live.

But I'm never asked about what I've found to be the trickiest part of polyamory, for me.

It's trusting your partner to make decisions.

I've seen some impressively complex polyamorous rule systems in my day, but it's impossible to cover everything. And, as most lawyers will tell you, it's not just about the rules but about how they're applied to real life scenarios.

Especially when two or more rules are in conflict with one another. Which happens with elaborate rule systems. Or maybe there aren't any established guidelines for this situation. People end up making judgement calls.

And that's what I've found to be key in all of this — selecting partners whose judgement I really trust. That I trust so much that I would trust them to pick other partners who will also exercise reasonable judgement. And those partners, so on.

The thing is? As I move away from people I know well, those who I personally select and trust, I move further and further towards that third bucket of control. I don't have a lot of control over who anybody else selects. And certainly not over what a telemour does or doesn't do.

So I select direct partners whose judgement I trust an awful lot. Who seem to make decisions as reasonable as my own, or maybe even better. Because I know that as we move down the line, the soundness of personal judgement may be diluted.

Accepting that Third Bucket, the Uncontrollable

That third bucket? The one you can't control? It's a killer.

If all else is equal in a polyamorous relationship, that third bucket is a bit larger than in a monogamous one. But that's only if you proceed on auto-pilot.

If you're doing it right, you bolster the first and second buckets as well as you can.

An important part of that is setting appropriate boundaries. And respecting the boundaries set by others.

Act ethically yourself. And don't forget to let others know what you need.

Emotional Ergonomics: There's No Should. You Feel How You Feel

A core principle in the field of ergonomics is that a workstation should be designed with the user's comfort in mind. The tools are laid out to serve the body. When we contort our bodies in an effort to match up with poorly aligned tools, productivity suffers. And repetitive strain injuries can follow.

When I worked for a large hospital system, I had to meet with an ergonomics consultant who examined my workspace. And I had to take an online module every six months to demonstrate that I understood: If you're hurting or strained, rearrange your office. Or get new equipment that adapts to you better.

It's old news, especially if you've ever worked an office job. We know better than to cram ourselves into a physical setup that won't work. To box ourselves in.

So why do we do it emotionally?

"I Shouldn't Feel This Way"

I can't tell you how many times I've heard other people say, "I shouldn't feel this way."

In the past, it was practically my catchphrase. Like one of those old talking toys that cycle through a list of lines when you pull the string:

"I shouldn't feel this way."

"I'm sorry."

"You know what I mean?"

"That probably sounds weird."

But the secret is: There's no should.

You feel how you feel.

If you're anything like me, you want it to make sense and be "reasonable," but there aren't universal standards for this stuff. We're flying through a modern world with stone age brains. Sometimes they act a little wacky.

You get to want and need whatever you want. Now, that doesn't mean that you'll always get those things or that other people are obligated to give them to you.

But it also doesn't mean that anyone should judge you for feeling the way you do. Not other people. And certainly not you.

And it doesn't mean that you need to cram your emotions into a space that's uncomfortably small and just expect them to fit.

Better Emotional Ergonomics

Try letting your emotions be free range. Let them have a recess to go out and play. Now this doesn't mean hulking out and destroying half the office. But instead, try a bit of mindfulness.

As you're feeling, note what the feeling is, without passing judgement. A famous analogy in mindfulness teaching is that it's like sitting on the side of a road and watching cars drive by. You note each one as they pass. But you don't get in any of the cars. You simply observe them.

Try this with your feelings. Observe them and just let them drive past.

And over time, if you find that you're consistently unhappy or perturbed about something, dig into why that is. Is there something you could change about the situation that would make it less unpleasant for you?

Whenever possible, find a way to make your environment optimally fit the emotional task. And when you want to work on challenging your feelings, don't try to un-feel them. Acknowledge them first. And then test them against the reality they're responding to.

Exercises to Try to Incorporate Mindfulness Into Your Daily Life

Pay close attention to something you do on a daily (or more than daily basis). When you're washing your hair in the shower, unloading the dishwasher, or taking a walk, focus intently on what you're doing. You may feel your mind wander. If it does, no big deal. Just redirect your attention back to the feeling of putting shampoo in your hair, the way that you stack plates, or the way that your feet roll when you walk.

1. Deep breathing. You don't need to sit yogi style for a half hour or more to take advantage of breath-based meditation. Take three or four deep breaths and pay attention to how those breaths feel. For maximum effect, do this multiple times a day, especially when you need to calm down or focus on a task that might be stressful.

2. Grounded sitting. Sit down in a chair and take note of how your body feels sitting in it. Put your hands down

flat on your lap or on whatever counter, desk, or table is nearby. How do your hands feel? If your mind wanders, don't worry about it. Just take a second and redirect your attention back to focusing on those sensations.

3. Focus on sounds. When you have an opportunity and it's safe to do so (you're not driving, are in a safe location and not in danger of falling asleep somewhere you shouldn't), close your eyes for a few moments and listen to the ambient sounds all around you. What kinds of sounds do you hear? Building noises? The whirring of fans? Birds singing? If there are people talking, try not to get caught up in the meanings of what they're saying but simply listen to the sound of their words. As with all of these exercises, if your mind wanders, don't fuss. Simply redirect your attention. You don't need to listen for very long. Thirty seconds might be enough. I find that two minutes are nearly always enough.

4. Emotional check-in. Ask yourself "How am I feeling?" Feel how the emotion sits in your body physically. No matter what that emotion is, don't judge yourself for it. Don't worry if it's right or wrong. Just name the emotion and feel how it physically sits you, as though that emotion were simply hands lying flat on the tabletop.

With all of these exercises, frequency is much more important than length. If you want to see benefits, many short mindfulness check-ins (even of 30 seconds or less) are much more effective than a half hour session once a day.

While you do these exercises, you might find that your mind wanders. This doesn't mean that you're doing a bad job or that you won't see benefit. It's very normal. Mindfulness is an exercise program for your emotions and attention. Just like it's normal to experience physical muscle fatigue when you start going to the gym, you're going to run into times when you feel like you're not good at the exercises.

This is normal. People often feel weak while they're building strength – whether that's physical or mental.

Mindfulness Application: Watch Out for the Ladder of Inference

Once you've begun to get the hang of fostering mindfulness within yourself (intrapersonal mindfulness), it's time to see if you can apply it to social situations (interpersonal mindfulness).

One way to start implementing this is to start paying attention to the ladder of inference.

The ladder of inference is a thinking process that we go through, without realizing that we do. The concept is attributed to Chris Argyris, a well-known organizational learning and development expert from Harvard Business School, and later popularized by Peter Senge [1].

At the bottom of the ladder of inference are facts and reality. Starting from experiencing these, we then climb up the ladder and go on to:

- Experience this reality through a selective filter based on our belief systems and our life experiences.

- Interpret what our filtered experiences mean.

- Apply our existing assumptions, sometimes without examining those assumptions.

- Form conclusions based on our interpretation of facts and our existing assumptions.

- Develop beliefs based on these conclusions we draw.

- Take action that seems correct to us because they are based on what we believe.

As one would expect, this process is recursive. It feeds on itself. What we believe biases us to look for things that solidify, rather than challenge, those beliefs (a.k.a, confirmation bias)[2].

By narrowing our selection of original information to consider (in alignment with our beliefs), we stack the odds that we'll come to similar conclusions in the future.

And after a while, instead of even climbing up the ladder, we jump right to conclusions.

Towards More Mindful Climbing

Now, I don't say this just to depress you. The more aware we are of the individual steps we have taken to reach a conclusion, and the more actively we check and challenge our belief system, the less likely we are to fall prey to the worst of its effects.

Here are some questions to ask yourself when you feel yourself slipping up the rungs:

Am I considering all the facts? What are some things that I didn't consider that I should?

What assumptions am I making? Are these assumptions reality based?

What beliefs are guiding me through this decision-making process? Are these beliefs well founded? Why or why not?

What data have I decided to focus on and why? What data have I ignored?

As you practice taking a second to slow down, make a note of which rungs you tend to skip past.

Consider talking through your reasoning with someone else, particularly someone who is comfortable enough to disagree with or correct you if there's something you're not seeing.

With sustained practice and time, you'll find that you're jumping to conclusions less — although I don't know anyone who doesn't slip up every once in a while (especially when it comes to our hot buttons).

Be Kind to Yourself

It's bad enough dealing with a nasty situation involving other people who are stressing you out. The last thing you want to do is make that worse.

Self-compassion is your friend here. Simply put, self-compassion is extending to yourself the same kindness, warmth, and understanding that you would show towards other people you care about. In other words, self-compassion involves being as good to ourselves as we would be to a dear friend.

Researcher Kristin Neff has devoted her life to studying self-compassion, how it works, and ways to foster it within ourselves. Her website self-compassion.org has a wealth of information on this research and resources for applying it to everyday life[3].

But here is one simple exercise you can do to build up self-compassion.

Would I Treat a Friend This Way?

Any time you are struggling with self-critical feelings over a difficult situation, ask yourself: If a friend were going through something similar, how would I treat them?

Compare this reaction to the way you're treating yourself. If you would treat your friend with more kindness than you're showing yourself, it's time to reevaluate.

Paying the Speeding Ticket: Why Self-Compassion Matters in Relationships

Self-compassion[4] is more important than self-esteem[5] when it comes to success in life and overall emotional well-being.

Self-compassion is not only important for our individual happiness. It's also vital in relationships.

The reason for this: People who are low in self-compassion? Often have trouble admitting to their mistakes.

This is especially true when they also have high self-esteem (helloooo narcissists[6]).

We Fight Harder When We View Mistakes as Life or Death

Think about it in legal terms.

The size of the fight we put up hinges greatly on what will happen if we don't defend ourselves.

Let's say we view something like a speeding ticket. We're likely to pay a small fine. A lot of us? If we can afford the ticket, we just pay it off. Get it out of our lives.

But if we're charged with a capital crime? And we're facing a life sentence or the death penalty? If we have the resources to fight that, you bet your life (literally) that we will.

When the consequences of being convicted are more severe, the defense makes more of an effort to avoid the charge.

And When We're Most Defensive? We'll Fight Dirty

If we're low in self-compassion, our mistakes can feel more like a capital crime than a speeding ticket.

And when making mistakes is so unacceptable to us that they feel like a capital charge? Our inner lawyer will come in and fight the good fight.

Deny. Rationalize. Do anything but confess and take responsibility. (Without an exhausting plea bargain process anyway.)

Those lowest in self-compassion may even launch a counterattack — not only refusing to make the mistakes that they made but also putting their partner on trial. Flipping everything around deftly so that there's a new defendant.

To Be Kind and Forgiving to the People in Our Lives, We Must Start with Ourselves

The sad thing is? No one is on trial. Especially not in a relationship. We're all imperfect. Mistakes are gonna happen. The only perfect person is one you don't know well enough yet.

Being kind and forgiving to our partners –and metamours – starts with us.

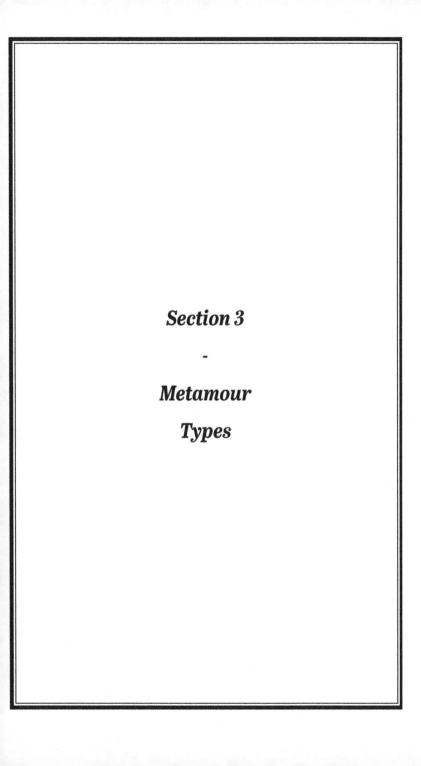

Section 3

-

Metamour

Types

Light and Dark - The Metamour Types

To confront a person with his shadow is to show him his own light. Once one has experienced a few times what it is like to stand judgingly between the opposites, one begins to understand what is meant by the self. Anyone who perceives his shadow and his light simultaneously see himself from two sides and thus gets in the middle.

-Carl Jung

It would be nigh impossible to create an all-inclusive list of all the ways that metamours can be difficult. What follows is an overview of some of the most common challenging dynamics I've encountered working as a relationship coach for polyamorous people.

Each type of problem metamour has its own section, and within each section, I first address the "shadow" side of that metamour type before looking at its other side, its "light" attributes.

This is because it's important to keep in mind that there's a duality to personality: What can be a difficult personality in one sense might also possess some strengths. Characteristics that can be troublesome in one context may be beneficial in another.

As I mentioned in the introduction, dealing with difficult metamours involves:

1. Changing the way that we interact with them

2. Changing how we perceive them and their actions

3. Learning better ways to cope with what will always bother us

Making sure to keep the "light" side of their personality in mind can help with all three of these.

Emphasizing their light side is by definition using the second strategy, changing how we perceive them and their actions. Changing the way we perceive them might in turn change the way we interact with them (#1). And doing so may make it easier to be more patient with them and emotionally cope with troubling behaviors (#3).

CARETAKER

PEOPLE PLEASER

I guess I'm a recovering people pleaser...is that okay?

Light

Very Supportive

Good at Exercising Self-Control

Respect Boundaries Set by Others

Dark

Won't Help Themselves

Take on Too Much

At Risk of Being Abused

The People Pleaser

"I'm a people pleaser," they say. "I can't help myself. When I see someone wants something, I have to give it to them. I need to make people happy." And it sounds like a good thing, at least on the surface. What could possibly be wrong with people pleasing?

Plenty, it turns out.

Focusing Solely on Pleasing Others Leaves Your Own Needs Unmet

People pleasers are conflict averse and afraid of troubling others. Because of these qualities, they often don't ask for help when they need it.

And forget about self-care. They spend so much of their time and attention catering to other's needs that their own go ignored.

All of this can contribute to a growing resentment. This resentment builds silently with no one — not even the people pleaser –realizing it's even happening until it's too late.

One day they suddenly snap, boiling over without any advance warning that they were even the slightest bit upset.

People Pleasing Is the Fast Track to Broken Promises

Because they have an incredibly difficult time saying "no" to people, people pleasers lack the ability to set healthy boundaries. They quickly become overextended. Committed to more than they can possibly fulfill, people pleasers are forced to break promises they never should have made in the first place.

They say that you can please some of the people all of the time, you can please all of the people some of the time, but you can't please all of the people all of the time.

And it's not only that you can't. You **shouldn't** try to please all of the people all of the time.

If a person's expectations are unreasonable, disappointing them is not only okay – it's the appropriate response. And the opposite is also true. Meeting those unreasonable expectations? Could very well be utterly inappropriate.

This is the kind of difficult metamour that I was.

When I entered into polyamorous relationships and especially once I became a busy hinge, I found that my former way of relating in romantic relationships (people pleasing to the point of emotional martyrdom) no longer worked with multiple people in the picture.

When Partner A wanted something, and Partner B wanted something that directly opposed that, I was forced to consider what I wanted. I had to learn to advocate for my preferences, even when they weren't universally popular. To discuss, negotiate, and compromise. And occasionally to go against the grain and decide to do something that only I wanted.

I became my own primary partner.

The Caretaker

On the other hand, people prone to people pleasing can also be thought of as caretakers.

Caretakers have excellent relationship skills. They're great at providing emotional support and exercising self-control. They anticipate the needs of others and will climb mountains to improve the lives of those they love.

This can be a wonderful thing. Caretakers have a great number of strengths. When dating other caretakers, the mutual support system is unshakable, solid, and wonderful. Helping people is generally gratifying and feels good.

However, caretakers are at risk of being abused by unscrupulous or selfish partners. They also may not take enough time or do enough for themselves. The big challenges for a caretaker are to learn how to set healthy boundaries and to make sure they don't skimp on self-care.

Caretakers also have a difficult time asking for support from others when they need it and making sure that they don't run themselves down helping others. They often won't recognize when they're being mistreated. So accustomed to taking care of others, some may even have troubling accepting support that they desperately need.

Many caretaker types grew up in environments where direct communication wasn't emotionally safe. This is sometimes referred to as Guess Culture. Let's take a closer look at that.

Ask Versus Guess Culture

Andrea Donderi[7] first identified the framework of Ask Culture and Guess Culture[8]:

> In some families, you grow up with the expectation that it's OK to ask for anything at all, but you gotta realize you might get no for an answer. This is Ask Culture.
>
> In Guess Culture, you avoid putting a request into words unless you're pretty sure the answer will be yes. Guess Culture depends on a tight net of shared expectations. A key skill is putting out delicate feelers. If you do this with enough subtlety, you won't even have to make the request directly; you'll get an offer. Even then, the offer may be genuine or pro forma; it takes yet more skill and delicacy to discern whether you should accept.
>
> All kinds of problems spring up around the edges. If you're a Guess Culture person...then unwelcome requests from Ask Culture people seem presumptuous and out of line, and you're likely to feel angry, uncomfortable, and manipulated.
>
> If you're an Ask Culture person, Guess Culture behavior can seem incomprehensible, inconsistent, and rife with passive aggression.
>
> Thing is, Guess behaviors only work among a subset of other Guess people -- ones who share a fairly specific set of expectations and signalling techniques. The farther you get from your own family and friends and subculture, the more you'll have to embrace Ask behavior. Otherwise you'll spend your life in a cloud of mild outrage at...the Cluelessness of Everyone.

If your metamour seems to come from a Guess Culture and you're from Ask Culture, this can cause all sorts of problems.

The key to breaking through this confusion is trying to make your metamour feel as safe as they can asking for things. Don't just give them an "out" when it comes to difficult tasks, give them in an "in" for getting perks or things they might seem to want. It might also be helpful if you can to introduce them to the Ask Versus Guess Culture framework and see what they have to say about it.

Questions to Ask This Metamour

- "Yes, but what do you want?"

- "If you didn't have to consider anybody else's feelings, what would you decide?"

Things to Try

- Don't just give this metamour an out. Give them ins. Make space for them to get what they want.

- Defer to this metamour if it isn't a big deal to you.

- Make small tweaks that make sharing time and resources easier, especially when it benefits both of you.

- Encourage your metamour to set and keep boundaries with you and others.

- Make an effort to let this metamour know that you respect, value, and want to hear their opinion.

#1 METAMOUR

BUTTINSKI

I like having metamours almost more than I like having partners. Let's be best friends!

Light

Good at Sharing Time and Attention

Compersion Masters

Very Friendly as a Metamour

Dark

Nosy

Poor Sense of Other's Boundaries

Struggles When Metamour Relationships Aren't Close

Buttinski

Buttinski Sign. It's arguably the thing that I find hardest about polyamory. And it's never what I'm asked about when people first learn I'm polyamorous. Usually, the most frequently asked question is something like "But don't you get jealous?" (The answer to that question incidentally is yes occasionally, but not all the time, and it's not the end of the world when/if that it happens.)

No, the thing that I struggle with the most as a poly person is butting in inappropriately. Into joyful situations, stressful ones, the works. I have to actively check myself to consider if I'm about to be a Buttinski. And I experience incredible frustration when others do it, cross boundaries inappropriately.

What's interesting about polyamory is that you will often find yourself stuck in the middle of things. Conflicts of interest crop up easily when different partners and metamours want different things from each other and from you (and you, from them). This is natural and nearly unavoidable. And at these times, all parties must endeavor to work as rationally, compassionately, and patiently as they can muster. When it works, it's a beautiful thing. When it doesn't? Holy hornbeam.

Given the difficulty and quasi inevitability of these occasional conflicts, it is vital to keep yourself out of elective hot water.

You have to understand what is and isn't your business. (Which can toooootally change depending on the nature of your agreements and the personalities of those involved. These are custom relationships, after all.)

That Fine Line Between Incredible Metamour and Buttinski

I will be the first to admit that I struggle with this. A big reason that I'm polyamorous is that I am very interested in other people.

The nice way of saying it: I've been fascinated by other people for as long as I can remember, what goes on inside their heads, why they do the things they do.

The other, less nice way: I'm nosy AF.

I feel a shit-ton of compersion. Love having metamours when they're good to my partners. Do what I can to make it easier for my partner to date others. And it's really hard to TMI me when talking about your other relationships.

But the last thing I want to do? Is end up chaperoning for my partner's other relationships. Looming over them at the school dance. On red alert for grinding or deep kissing in the shadowy reaches of the gym.

Privacy Please

While an overall atmosphere of transparency is a wonderful thing in polyamory (as it can promote understanding and build trust), there is such a thing as taking it too far. Some privacy can be very important for building intimacy in romantic relationships.

After all, some plants can't handle full sun.

The last time I did a robust OkCupid sweep, I corresponded with a young man who apologized after one period of silence for taking so long, explaining that his girlfriend had to review and approve all outgoing messages to other partners, and she had been quite busy with professional obligations and hadn't gotten around to it.

Granted, there weren't any sparks to speak of (I just ended up giving the guy poly advice he asked for), and that probably would have died on its own, but I can't imagine opening up with authentic vulnerability with such a chaperone structure in the picture. Still, he seemed a bit upset when I declined to pursue a relationship, so I imagine I'm not the only one not keen to forge connections under such a microscope.

Good Boundaries: It Isn't Your Relationship Even When It Affects You

And there's another way I see Buttinski Sign damaging polyamorous relationship systems: The poor boundaries that often accompany the behavior.

As I mentioned in the chapter on Polyamory and Boundaries, poor boundaries aren't just about letting people walk all over you. They can also involve succumbing to your Inner Buttinski.

A lot of people get into poly because they easily connect with others. And sometimes we risk latching on in a way that's not helpful. To anyone.

#1 Metamour

Some people just really love having metamours! If they could, they'd wear a T-shirt that says "#1 Metamour" just as proudly as folks sport one that says "World's Greatest Dad."

For a #1 metamour, metamour relationships aren't just a side effect of being polyamorous; instead they're one of the biggest upsides of polyamory.

However, being close friends with a metamour can lead to uncomfortable conflicts of interest for the #1 metamour when you fight with your mutual partner.

In these situations, it's important for a #1 metamour to remember that it's not their relationship and avoid butting in inappropriately.

#1 Metamours also struggle with feelings of disappointment in situations where they don't hit it off with a metamour due to personality conflicts.

And it can be very difficult for #1 metamours when their partners break up with a beloved metamour. The loss of the closeness of the metamour relationship can be devastating. And even if the friendship survives the breakup, it can be awkward balancing the concerns of the partner and the ex-metamour, particularly if the breakup was contentious.

But there are definite benefits to this type. Since #1 metamours don't view their metamours as competition, they tend to be good at sharing time and attention. Generally, this results in less conflict in a poly web.

Rather than viewing their metamours as competitors, a #1 metamour see them as new friends and new opportunities for support — to them, their other partners, or both.

Questions to Ask Yourself

If you feel like your metamour is meddling in your relationship with your partner:

- Are they trying to protect our partner?

- Are they trying to help me somehow?

- What bothers me most about their behavior?

- If things could be different, how would they ideally play out?

Things to Try

- Tell your metamour you know that they're coming from a good place.

- If you haven't already, explicitly set boundaries.

- For situations where your boundaries have been violated after they're explicitly set, consider an accountability talk (see "How to Have an Accountability Talk" on page 141 for tips on how to do that).

ACCOUNTABILITY EXPERT
BLAME-SHIFTING NINJA

Just so everyone's perfectly clear, I did nothing wrong.

Light

Adept at Detecting Relationship Problems

Addresses Conflicts

Won't Ignore Mistakes

Dark

Can Get Caught Up in the Blame Game

May Fall Prey to Black and White Thinking Struggles

Has Trouble Taking Responsibility

Blame-Shifting Ninja

To err is human, right?

Not for this metamour.

Nothing is ever their fault. Maybe it's always your fault. Maybe it's your shared partner's. But one thing is for certain: This metamour never does anything wrong. When something unfortunate happens, it's always due to someone else. And they're quick to point it out.

Oh blame. Few things are less productive and more divisive than the blame game.

Sometimes it's obvious when you're being blamed. "This is all your fault."

But unfortunately it's not always so easy to sort it out. Blame can be rather insidious and wear many more acceptable masks. It can sound like the following:

- You made me…

- You gave me no choice but to…

- Because of you, I…

But the priorities here are clear: The top priority in the blame game is to figure out who is wrong and let them know. Not to actually fix the problem or find ways to prevent it from happening again in the future.

Accountability Expert

Blaming people is different than holding them accountable for what they do.

When we focus on accountability, we stress keeping agreements and being respectful to one another. Conversely, blaming is a highly emotional process that stresses discrediting the blamed party.

An accountability framework assumes that everyone is capable of making mistakes or falling short of commitments.

Researcher Carol Dweck has studied the field of motivation extensively, and her work has uncovered that when it comes to learning, people tend to either espouse a growth mindset or a fixed mindset (also known sometimes in her work as incremental and entity).

According to Dweck[9]:

> For twenty years, my research has shown that the view you adopt for yourself profoundly affects the way you lead your life. It can determine whether you become the person you want to be and whether you accomplish the things you value. How does this happen? How can a simple belief have the power to transform your psychology and, as a result, your life?

> Believing that your qualities are carved in stone — the fixed mindset — creates an urgency to prove yourself over and over. If you have only a certain amount of intelligence, a certain personality, and a certain moral character — well, then you'd better prove that you have a healthy dose of them. It simply wouldn't do to look or feel deficient in these most basic characteristics.

[...]

I've seen so many people with this one consuming goal of proving themselves — in the classroom, in their careers, and in their relationships. Every situation calls for a confirmation of their intelligence, personality, or character. Every situation is evaluated: Will I succeed or fail? Will I look smart or dumb? Will I be accepted or rejected? Will I feel like a winner or a loser?...

There's another mindset in which these traits are not simply a hand you're dealt and have to live with, always trying to convince yourself and others that you have a royal flush when you're secretly worried it's a pair of tens. In this mindset, the hand you're dealt is just the starting point for development. This growth mindset is based on the belief that your basic qualities are things you can cultivate through your efforts. Although people may differ in every which way — in their initial talents and aptitudes, interests, or temperaments — everyone can change and grow through application and experience.

Do people with this mindset believe that anyone can be anything, that anyone with proper motivation or education can become Einstein or Beethoven? No, but they believe that a person's true potential is unknown (and unknowable); that it's impossible to foresee what can be accomplished with years of passion, toil, and training.

A focus on accountability embraces the growth mindset: All of us, even good people, are fallible, and relationships are a learning process.

In contrast, blame assumes that our character is called into question when we run into snags. We are only so good at having relationships. Or at being considerate. Or detail oriented.

Whatever quality is being evaluated. And any isolated mistake can shine the light on our inherent, and immutable, deficiencies. In the fixed mindset of blame, our number one priority is to make sure that mistake reflects on the other person and not us.

When playing the blame game we're operating under a number of irrational beliefs:

- When something goes wrong, it's important to identify someone else who is responsible for the error and make sure it is clear that they have caused the problem.

- Because of this person's wrongdoing, they are owed less respect and we can treat them in ways that are disrespectful. For example, calling them names or ignoring them.

- Accepting any personal responsibility for the unfortunate situation is unacceptable because it would open us up to disrespectful treatment.

Blame frames ourselves and others as falling into a dichotomy: We are either flawed or perfect.

Accountability, however, focuses not on who committed the error but what can be learned from it and how things can be improved to avoid similar errors in the future. In accountability, there is plenty of middle ground. The goal of an accountability discussion isn't perfection, but improvement.

Questions to Ask Yourself

- Do I have a fixed or a growth mindset?

- Some people find that their opinion of this changes over time. That's okay. If your opinion has changed, when did that change and why?

- Think of a time where someone blamed you for something in a way that made it hard for you to talk things over and solve the problem. How could that conversation have gone differently and been more productive? What would an accountability talk look like in that same situation?

- Think of a time where you were quick to blame someone else. Consider the same questions: How could that conversation have gone differently and been more productive? What would an accountability talk look like in that same situation?

Things to try

- Own responsibility for your own mistakes.

- Reframe personal responsibility not as a need for perfection but as a commitment to learning from your own mistakes and those of others.

- Refuse to play into the blame game via retaliation or disrespectful behavior.

- Model accountability instead of blame as a communication framework with your metamour (and others in your life). Please see "How to Have an Accountability Talk" on page 141 for more information on ways to do this.

OPEN BOOK

DRAMA LLAMA

Yeah, so everything's messed up again. I hate to ask, but is there any way you could help me out?

Light

You Never Have to Guess What They're Thinking

Have Little Trouble Asking for Support They Need

Less Likely to Ignore Conflict

Dark

Frequent Crises Can Be Disruptive

A Hot Freaking Mess

Constant Interpersonal Conflict

Drama Llama

We all know someone who seems like they've always having a crisis. It can be difficult enough if you have a friend who just can't seem to keep it together. You want to be there for them as much as possible, but it seems like every five minutes you have to rush in and save them from some type of mess. Or support them through a dramasplosion that feels like it could have been very easily avoided.

But when it's your metamour, it can be doubly disruptive, especially when those crises leak over into your time with your partner. Or you can see the emotional toll it's taking on your partner.

We all go through a rough spot every now and then, but the Drama Llama doesn't just go through difficult times. They've basically built their house there. It's where they live.

Let's face it: The Drama Llama is a hot freaking mess.

This can be for a number of reasons, including:

- Difficulty managing their own emotions

- Difficulty managing their lives as far as practical responsibilities

- Constant interpersonal conflict with others

- Maladaptive coping strategies like substance use and abuse

Some Drama Llamas also have trouble with inappropriately oversharing their problems and gossiping. See the chapter on the Gossip / Connector (page 113) for more information on that).

Open Book

And yet, a person with no filter can be one of the most refreshing people we know.

There's nothing wrong with needing emotional or practical support from time to time, and it's important to be able to safely express the desire for support to those closest to us.

Sadly, "drama" has evolved to be a clever catch-all label for a number of undesirable qualities and behaviors from people in our life.

Merriam-Webster defines drama as "a state, situation, or series of events involving interesting conflict of forces.[10]"

Interesting. Not necessarily negative.

No, when drama becomes irksome is when it results in disruption.

And sure, maybe some of that conflict is disruptive – but avoiding every conflict isn't good either. That can also lead to disruption, sometimes even more serious than if those little conflicts had been dealt with in the moment.

What's Your Conflict Style?

"Conflict is inevitable, but combat is optional."

-Max Lucado[11]

There are worse things than conflict, including perpetually running away from one you need to address. The trouble of course lies in the reality that being honest and resolving conflicts are both much easier in theory than they are in practice.

I have lived with this difference when I was newly polyamorous.

"So… How do you make it work?" I asked my friend after she told me she was polyamorous and explained what that was.

"Simple," she said. "Open, honest communication."

And that would become our mantra. As my partner and I discussed opening up and as he and I came to date this same friend.

It was beautiful, elegant in its simplicity. The one law that we would come back to. Were you engaging in open, honest communication? If not, why not? Get open. Get honest.

And a lot of the times? It worked.

But sometimes, not so much.

Being honest with other people begins with self-honesty. And unfortunately, even the most self-aware and courageous people can occasionally run into situations where they falter with their assessment of their emotional state, their needs. Self-honesty is not a one-time fix. Or a static ability. It is an ongoing process, one that we must exercise to improve. It is not easy. Some realizations are unpleasant and painful. But long term, owner-ship of these is a freeing proposition. Especially being free of the quest to be perfect.

But let's say everyone involved is reasonably good with self-honesty, and the situation is one where people aren't defensive and are sharing well.

That's it, right? We've shared what we feel. Conflict solved?

Nope.

It's easy to pare conflict resolution down to a simple binary of "not addressing conflict" versus "addressing conflict," but in reality, there a variety of ways that we can handle conflict.

One popular model by researchers Kilmann and Thomas[12] breaks styles of conflict resolution down into 5 categories:

1. Avoiding.

2. Accommodating.

3. Collaborating.

4. Competing.

5. Compromising

Avoiding

This is when you attempt to resolve a conflict by simply avoiding the issue.

When It's Used: When the issue is trivial. Or when engaging in the situation will result in damage no matter your actions.

One place I see people use this frequently is when two of their friends are fighting with one another. A common practice is to refuse to take sides or comment on the conflict and to remain neutral.

Another scenario is when you disagree with someone about something that doesn't matter a lot to you, to them, or both. Not worth bringing up.

People have also used this tactic effectively when a conflict arises that seems to be an isolated incident. If it's only happened one time, and people all seem to be acting in good faith, it can be appropriate to not raise the issue.

Drawbacks: Since this is a tactic that's low cost in time and energy and plays into most people's natural fears and negative perceptions of conflict, it's often overused and applied inappropriately. This can result in larger conflicts that are more difficult to solve.

Additionally, if a one-time isolated event becomes a pattern but was not at least brought up to other person or people involved, they might not remember the initial incident. And in this scenario, you may very well find yourself in an argument about whether something did or didn't happen. One that's impossible to really prove. Cognitive science has well demonstrated that even the best memories are imprecise[13], and the boxing match of Yes You Did versus No I Didn't is exhausting. Spoiler: Everyone loses.

Accommodating

This is when you give in and accept what others want, even if this comes at great expense to yourself.

When It's Used: When you believe that the other person or people involved know more than you and has a better solution. Or when you feel like the potential cost to you is not worth the damage to the relationship.

Caregiver polyamorous hinges and people pleasers do this a lot (see People Pleaser / Caretaker on page 53 for more information).

However, handling a conflict with an accommodating style can also be rather strategic and savvy. It can be used appropriately on a current conflict that you may be able to leverage that good will into getting something else you care more about.

Drawbacks: You don't get what you want. And it may cause you a great amount of consternation and inconvenience.

Additionally, if you are wrong in your belief that the others have superior knowledge and solutions, the situation can worsen. This can end up damaging the relationship more in the long term.

Collaborating

This is a style in which everyone involved contributes to the discussion, and the main goal for everyone involved is a win-win scenario.

When It's Used: Complicated situations where the right course of action isn't clear, and the outcome is important.

Drawbacks: It requires a high level of trust and patience among all parties. It's also very consuming of both time and energy.

Additionally, establishing "all those involved" can be a sticky point. This rears its head often in polyamorous situations. Who should be part of the problem-solving process for a specific conflict? The direct parties involved in an incident? Metamours? Telemours (your metamours' partners)?

There's no one right answer for all situations

Erring in either direction can have consequences: Involving unnecessary people can result in "too many cooks in the kitchen." The conflict can take longer to solve and be solved with a poorer solution (due to the potential inclusion of perspectives with limited firsthand experience of any of the important tenets of the conflict).

On the other hand, omitting people crucial to the achievement of the win-win scenario can cause resentment and lead to incomplete solutions.

It's a tricky balance.

In general, I'm a big fan of this style and consider it a gold standard of conflict resolution — however, I have seen it pan out horribly when not applied well.

Competing

If Collaborating is seeking a win-win scenario, Competing is its shadow: A strategy that achieves win-lose. You impose your solution with limited to no openness to the input of others, even if it your solution comes at great cost to others.

When It's Used: Steamroller metamours have a tendency to approach conflict this way (see the Steamroller / Activator on page 107 for more information). It's not a secret I'm not a huge fan of competition and prefer social facilitation[14]. But Competing style does have its place. It can be appropriate to use this style when a decision needs to be made rather quickly, for example, an emergency situation that requires immediate action and in which you are reasonably sure that you are doing the right thing.

Drawbacks: Zero sum thinking (the belief that life is a game in which when one person "wins," another has to "lose") is terrible for your psychological health[15]. Overuse of this strategy can strain relationships and lead to resentment and even retaliation. In addition, many conflicts will be improperly solved and addressed with insufficient solutions.

Compromising

The final style of conflict resolution is the lose-lose situation. In this style, no one really achieves what they want.

When It's Used: While it sounds like a real bummer, this strategy can be appropriate when a temporary solution needs to be in place until a better one can be implemented. No one is thrilled about it. But it's better than avoiding the situation altogether.

Drawbacks: People sometimes fall prey to using this style when in fact Collaborating would produce a better solution because they are discouraged by frustration, undervalue the importance of the problem, or underestimate the amount of time and resources they have to solve the problem.

Questions to Ask

Time for a little bit of that good old self-honesty: Think about how you have addressed conflicts in the past.

- Do you have a default style for dealing with conflict?

- Can you think of some situations where you used one style and some situations where you used another? What were the outcomes? How did it go?

- Consider the alternative styles in those same scenarios. How might have the outcome been different?

- How is your current style of conflict management affecting your relationship (positively and negatively)?

Things to Try

- Trying a different style of conflict resolution with your metamour

- Picking your battles. Focus on only the crises that they're having that directly impact your life and ignoring the rest (as much of a mess as it might be)

- Setting boundaries with your metamour and shared partner around any crises that directly impact your relationship. For example, if your partner is frequently late to things you've planned together because your metamour is late or having foreseeable difficulties, then it's entirely appropriate to draw a line that it's unacceptable and to work on solutions to prevent it from happening. Please see "Polyamory and Boundaries" on page 29 for more information.

ORGANIZER

CONTROL FREAK

Let me handle that for you. I got this.

Light

Can Make Order from Chaos

Prepares Thorough Contingency Plans

Less Likely to Ignore Conflict

Dark

Can Be Critical of Others

Prone to Double Binds and Scapegoating

Has a Hard Time Trusting Others

Control Freak

There are many ways that people engage in controlling behavior. Some of them can be quite subtle, others terribly obvious.

This isn't a complete list, but as you can see, there are a lot of ways that people can try to control others:

1. Constant criticism, even about little issues. While there may be legitimate concerns, raising problems on too frequent a basis keeps other people on the defensive and makes them too busy to raise any concerns of their own they may have.

2. Saying things like "If you really loved me, you…" or "someone who was really poly would…"

3. Threats – to cut off privileges, to self-harm, and in extreme cases even threats of violence

4. Using guilt to get their way

5. Expecting you to read their mind, remaining unhappy until other people can guess what they want

6. Keeping score – maintaining a mental tally of every good deed they've done and bringing it up in conversations as a reason why they should get something in return

7. Giving gifts or doing kind things as a way to create a "debt" so they can demand a favor in return later

8. Snooping or requiring complete transparency about issues that would be reasonable to keep private (see "If Your Calendar…" on page 87)

9. Not respecting request for adequate time alone

10. Not giving you the benefit of the doubt – assuming something is your fault when there isn't enough "evidence" in order to make that kind of assessment

11. Exhausting you via constant arguments so that you'll give up and they "win"

12. Belittling you for your values

13. Teasing with "jokes" that have a very insensitive and hurtful undertone

14. Not being open to your ever expressing your point of view

15. Never agreeing or pretending that they do not understand others in conversation (see below in "Controlling by Not Understanding")

16. Frequently interrupting you in conversation

17. Pressuring you to engage in substance abuse

18. Isolating someone from social supports – friends, family, other lovers, etc.

19. Asking many questions, especially ones that are designed to embarrass the other person or make them look bad

20. Putting people in double binds (see "How to Know If You're a Scapegoat" on page 84)

21. Moving the goalposts. No matter how well you do something, they don't give you kudos. Instead they insist that you haven't done it well enough and quickly redefine success as something greater or immediately assign you a more difficult task.

22. Using a small concession to take greater advantage of you[16]. This is similar to the old saying "give an inch and they'll take a mile."

23. Pressuring you to respond or make a decision before you've had adequate time to think over matters

24. Employing the silent treatment

Going into depth on each of them is beyond the scope of this book, so I'll focus on just a few of these behaviors in greater detail.

How to Know If You're a Scapegoat

We all mess up from time to time. We're human. And it can be especially hard getting called out when we make a mistake, doubly so when it's by someone we care about. But if we do hurt someone we're close to, it's good for them to tell us so we can do better.

Except sometimes the criticism isn't valid. Maybe we didn't do it. Maybe they're confused. And maybe they're just being a big old jerk and using you as a scapegoat for their insecurities.

The story of the scapegoat originates in the book of Leviticus, and it's quite literally as it sounds. In order to atone for the community's sins, a goat would be exiled to the desert, to fend for itself on the harsh landscape.

Poor goat. Goats are adorable. Clearly you don't want to be this goat.

The surest sign that someone is trying to blame you for things that aren't your fault: They're putting you into double binds.

A double bind is when a person sends out two different messages, both of which conflicts with the other. This causes situations where no matter what you're doing, you're going to do "the wrong thing" and be criticized. A double bind is also known as "being between a rock and a hard place" and "damned if you do, damned if you don't." No matter what you do, you're a terrible person.

Double binds are a huge source of confusion, anxiety, and stress. They are often used as a form of control without open coercion. The fact that they are so confusing makes them difficult to address to or resist.

If someone is putting you into double binds repeatedly, it is emotional abuse.

One minute they're criticizing you for talking too much. The next they're saying you don't talk enough. If you point out this contradiction and ask what they right amount of talking would be, they criticize and invalidate you for asking for clarification:

"You're so dramatic."

"I shouldn't have to tell you something so obvious."

"Don't go into therapist mode on me."

"Ooo, someone's sensitive."

"That's not what I said. It helps if you listen. Maybe if you stopped talking so much and listened instead, you'd actually hear what people say."

The list goes on, basically whatever they can think of in the moment that they know will bother you.

The saddest part is that survivors of emotional abuse are especially vulnerable to this tactic. The same personality traits that make survivors resilient also make it hard for other people to understand them, and so many survivors develop insecurities that they're damaged and deserve more criticism.

In The Survivor Personality, Al Siebert writes[17]:

> Survivors puzzled me at first. They are serious and humorous, hard-working and lazy, self-confident and self-critical. They are not one way or the other, they are both one way and the other...biphasic personality traits increase survivability by allowing a person to be one way or its opposite in any situation or to fall somewhere along the continuum in between the two extremes. To have biphasic traits is to be more adaptable rather than being either one way or another. It is to be proud and humble, selfish and unselfish, cooperative and rebellious
>
> If you look at someone who does not handle life well, it is often because he always thinks, feels, or acts in only one way and would never consider the opposite.
>
> Many people with opposing or counterbalanced personality traits have been told something is wrong with them. People with rigid thinking can't handle complex people very well, and often view them as defective...it is healthy, not sick, to have two opposite feelings.

So what to do if you feel like someone is putting you in double binds? Simple.

Point out the contradiction, politely. It could just be a miscommunication issue. Assume good will. Observe their reaction.

If they continue to double bind, criticize, or invalidate you, especially if they escalate, then this is a serious issue. If this happens repeatedly, then it's emotional abuse, and you should seriously rethink your relationship with them, whether that means going to therapy or cutting off contact.

Life is far too short to waste on people who want to rake you over the coals for things you didn't even do.

"If Your Calendar Shows That You're Available, I Expect You to Be Here"

"I looked at your calendar. There wasn't anything on it," Michelle said.

"Ah," I said, not sure where she was going. She was right of course. But this observation hardly seemed noteworthy.

She sighed, and the tension in that sigh was unmistakable. "I went up to your room because I wanted to talk to you, and you weren't there."

"I got asked last minute to go hang out with a group of people. It sounded fun," I said.

"Why wasn't it on your calendar?" she said.

I stared at her. "Because it was last minute," I said.

Michelle rolled her eyes.

"It wasn't a date," I said.

"It doesn't matter," she said. "If your calendar shows that you're available, I expect you to be here."

That moment sticks with me now because of how surreal it felt. I'd spent considerable effort overcoming my insecurities, honing my communication skills, and adapting to polyamory only to be confronted with these kinds of demands.

As time wore on, it became more and more evident that Michelle, my boyfriend Rob's wife, didn't just want a heads up for potential new romantic entanglements, or even to always have a sense of where I was on any given evening, but a say in who I could and couldn't be friends with.

It struck me as bizarre. Polyamory had been a rough adjustment for me, but I did the work because I loved the benefits that came with it: An increased sense of autonomy and a fun life.

Michelle was supposedly polyamorous. Had even had a serious boyfriend of several years. And I was far from the first woman Rob had been involved with since their marriage had opened.

And yet, here Michelle was trying to control me in ways that I would never accept in a monogamous relationship or a friend. It felt like being parented.

Controlling by Not Understanding

I've learned to pay special attention to people who are uncomfortable when their own words are repeated back to them.

Healthy functional communication, especially during times of conflict, requires that both parties repeat and paraphrase what the other has said. Counselors train to do this, and many good listeners learn this intuitively. However, a very common controlling habit is when a person refuses to accept any paraphrase and may even reject direct quotes of what they've just said to you. You can repeat their exact words back, and they tell you, "That's not what I said."

You may even find that they argue one thing, you acknowledge it, and they turn around immediately and argue the opposite, putting you into double binds. It's almost as though they're on the run from you. In a way, they are.

Since the goal of communication is ultimately to understand one another, if they refuse to let you understand their point of view, then in a twisted sense, they "win." And wearing you out through your efforts to connect with them is a one-two punch. You become so exhausted that you don't have time to make any points of your own.

On its own, this controlling habit stops short of abuse. However, it's definitely a good wake-up call. It may just be a signal to evaluate the relationship and look for other patterns that might be problematic. One way you can test the ability to address the behavior is politely pointing it out when it happens and observing their reaction. It's best to do this in an undramatic fashion. Assume good will until proven otherwise.

If they deny or dismiss the behavior, then you may want to limit contact with them, if you can.

Keep in mind that repeat offenders may find it tough to break the habit. This is because many times people deal with anxiety through subtly controlling or critical behavior. As a result, they can be very invested in repeating those patterns, as they use them to cope.

The Organizer

> That horrifying moment when you're looking for adult, then realize you're an adult. So you look for an older adult, someone successfully adulting…an adultier adult.

-Internet meme

The Control Freak can be beyond aggravating. However, there's a flipside to the desire to control: The Organizer.

The Organizer can be many things: A preparedness guru. An efficient tidier who effortlessly flings chaos into neat little bento boxes where it can no longer harm anyone.

They take adulting[18] to new heights, making it into an artform. The adultiest adult on the block.

If I lose my eyes, I can see my own Organizer – that person I know who if they whisk me away at a moment's notice, I can trust that they'll get me home safely. Because even if we're going on an adventure, they'll have thought to pack enough snacks. And they've investigated every contingency plan and prepared for it.

Where a control freak may ignore personal boundaries and exercise control over others in a way that's inappropriate, an organizer takes that same anxiety and channels it into controlling external factors in a way that's boundary appropriate.

The same traits that can lend themselves to manipulation and abuse can be applied in a way that's good for everyone. The key difference is respecting the boundaries of those around you.

Questions to Ask Yourself

If you find yourself face to face with a control freak, ask yourself the following questions:

- What boundaries are they violating?

- What specific behaviors are the most bothersome?

- Think of all the people you know. Who would you say is most organized – or, if you prefer, who is the "adultiest adult?"

- Why do you say that? What qualities do they possess? What behaviors do they perform?

Things to Try

- Directly asking to be part of the plan-making

- Suggesting alternative plans

- When discussing frustrations with this metamour, focus on discussing the specific behaviors that are bothering you in a gentle, even-handed way (please see "How to Have an Accountability Talk" on page 141 for more help with this)

DAREDEVIL

RULE BREAKER

Rules were made to be broken.

Light

Dynamic Personality

Independent Thinker

Adventurous and Spontaneous

Dark

Takes Terrible Risks

Violates Relationship Agreements

Always Pushing the Limits

Rule Breaker

Many long-time polyamorous folks argue against setting rules in your relationships and instead recommend framing them as agreements.

The rule breaker doesn't do well with either.

They push the limits of whatever has been agreed upon as acceptable behavior.

What this looks like will vary based on the nature of the agreements that they're violating, but here are some common transgressions:

- Not implementing appropriate safer sex measures (not using barriers, engaging in intercourse with partners whose status is unknown or risking pregnancy through lack of appropriate contraception, etc.)

- Not properly notifying their other partners that they've taken on other partners within the specific timeframe (for some agreements, this is before seeking other partners, for some this is after it happens)

- If they've agreed to give permission before doing something, not asking that permission and just doing it (depending on the agreement, this could be going out on a romantic date, kissing, making out, having sex, or becoming "official" as a relationship, etc.).

Certain relationship agreements are very short. Taking a page from Google's old corporate motto "Don't be evil," one couple I knew had the sole dictum: "Don't be a jerk."

Sometimes agreements are a bit lengthier. Mine are usually longer than a single sentence – but typically have been able to be captured on a single sheet of paper.

But they can be much longer, depending on the personalities of those involved and the number and specificity of behavioral expectations from all involved.

And some polyamorous relationship systems have very formalized and regimented patterns of acceptable conduct. One guy I knew had to go on one date a month with a new partner for six months until they were allowed to kiss this new person.

This guideline was written up by his two partners precisely because he tended to be a bit of a Rule Breaker. They basically wrote the rules knowing that he had a propensity to push limits, and as a way of reining him in, they wrote the rules stricter than what they needed to happen – a bit like telling your chronically late friend that the party is a half an hour earlier than it actually is, knowing that they're much more likely to arrive on time that way.

Did he then go on to violate this extremely strict agreement? Yes, he did. Repeatedly. But the practical consequences of his breaches of trust were greatly diminished. And for them, that was enough.

Would it have been something that I would choose for myself? Probably not. But I watched with amazement from a safe distance how his partners had engineered this (perhaps dubious) fix…and seemingly without his ever catching on.

Daredevil

Would it be better if he had just followed the rules? Most certainly.

But they managed this workaround that got the job done in the end, and near as I could tell, they were all happy about it.

When I spoke with his partners, I observed that it must be very frustrating to have to deal with that kind of limit-testing behavior. "I'm not sure I'd want to put up with that myself," I said.

"It's just part of who he is," one of his partners insisted. "And besides it comes with perks."

"Perks?"

She told me that her partner was a very exciting dynamic person, and while initially she had been rather hurt by his propensity to push the limits, that she'd come to realize that this desire to break rules was linked to other parts of who he was that she did enjoy.

"Such as?"

He was a very independent thinker, she said. After being married to a doormat for a decade and seeing how her ex had been pushed around and the problems it caused, she preferred this new challenge. Plus, her new beau was spontaneous, lively, fun. He was adventurous, even a bit of a daredevil – qualities that sometimes came in conflict with rules.

And besides, he seemed to be doing better as time went on. It was taking a bit for the structure to settle in, but he was obviously trying to abide by his agreement, even if he sometimes still messed up.

And the aftermath when he did mess up on the way to getting better at managing multiple relationships (and the agreements that can accompany them) was considerably less damaging in the short term than when he'd had fewer restrictions.

That said, a metamour who repeatedly violates relationship agreements can be quite a serious matter. Not only does it undermine trust, but it can put the safety and emotional wellbeing of others at risk. This can affect not just your shared partner and you, but bad enough relationship agreement violations can cause a ripple effect and cause inconvenience and harm to your partners and even their partners' partners.

So while my friends may have worked out their own solution in an unorthodox way, they did so voluntarily and in a clear-eyed fashion. Violated relationship agreements are not something you should have to tolerate from a metamour or a partner if you don't want to.

Many relationships have ended because of this.

Please see "How to Have an Accountability Talk" on page 141 for help on how to have conversations about broken commitments.

Questions to Ask Yourself

- What are the consequences for violating the relationship agreements that apply to me?

- Could I forgive someone for violating our relationship agreement? If so, what factors would influence my ability to forgive and forget – or at least work with them to do better?

Things to try

- Being upfront, clear, and direct with any partners and metamours about the expectations you have regarding your relationship agreement

- Addressing violated relationship agreements within an accountability framework (please see How to Have an Accountability Talk for more information)

- Fostering open communication and an environment that make it easy for someone to be honest when they have made a mistake

- Being kind to yourself if you make the decision that you cannot have a metamour who perpetually violates relationship agreements, even if that means you can't see your shared partner anymore

GUARDIAN
SECRET SEX POLICE

I'm not letting anyone else put my own health or safety at risk.

Light

Promotes Sexual Safety

Protector of the Web/Polycule

Responsibility Oriented

Dark

Invades Privacy

May Raise STI Risk Objections to Mask Own Insecurities

Can Be Hypocritical in Own Behavior

Secret Sex Police

Once upon a time, I moved cross country from Maine to Ohio, leaving a girlfriend I loved very much back home. She and I missed each other, but she was really supportive of my choice and genuinely happy for me. All in all, she handled my moving away extremely well.

We continued to talk with one another frequently over chat. My girlfriend had always been a bit of a voyeur and was really curious about my sex life out in Ohio. She asked me questions so regularly about what I was up to that I created a special Google Calendar filter for her called "Bedpost," joking tongue-in-cheek that it was the place where I put all the notches in my bedpost.

In this filter, I'd record who I had sex with, in what position, and various other details for my girlfriend's licentious pleasure. It was all in good fun – and a bit silly – and I got the consent of my sex partners that they were was okay with me sharing those details with her. They were used to my girlfriend and I over-sharing with one another anyway.

My partners were fine. But my metamour wasn't. Everything changed when she got wind of Bedpost. My metamour demanded that I add her. And the first thing she did was read over my recent activity and figure out that our mutual partner hadn't told her about a sexual encounter we'd had and concluded he'd lied to her by not mentioning it.

I found this bizarre since they'd been poly for several years by this point, I was serious with our shared partner and openly fluid bonded with him, and my metamour and boyfriend had no such rule that he needed to clear or notify each encounter – at least not that I knew anyway.

Regardless, my metamour used the information she found on my calendar to harass him and start a long and nasty argument.

I shut down Bedpost not long after, even though it disappointed my girlfriend back home because my metamour used that info against our shared partner.

Not only that, but my metamour additionally criticized the manner in which I documented my sex life, complaining that I failed to record the time of day the encounters occurred.

The Curious Case of Vigilante Girl

When I think of Secret Sex Police, I often think of Vigilante Girl, an acquaintance who had a fairly contentious breakup with her boyfriend.

Vigilante Girl was very upset with this newly ex-boyfriend because she stated that he hadn't used gloves when he had fingered another one of his partners in their separate play session. She let everyone know what had happened and that he was a jerk who had jeopardized her health by this act, which in essence violated her consent for taking on that level of risk.

The trouble was that by every account (including hers), they hadn't talked about this specific act prior to this happening. Furthermore, I personally witnessed her giving unprotected fellatio to a new partner with unknown STI status (at a wild party we were both attending) without consulting anyone, so I could see how her boyfriend could have made the assumption that this was okay.

This spiraled into an ongoing saga of melodramatic proportions where this Vigilante Girl decided that her gloveless newly ex-boyfriend was an unsafe person and tried to get him banned from any social event she even had the slightest interest of attending.

Surprisingly, she got a couple of major social capital holders in our local poly/kink community to jump aboard the Ban Train, and he did indeed get disinvited/banned from some parties. This caused some serious hurt for her ex-boyfriend's other partners, who were forced into the choice between attending things without him or not going to the events themselves (both sucky choices).

That would have been bad enough. But then, months after they had broken up, one of this ex-boyfriend's play partners tested positive for some sort of herpes, and somehow Vigilante Girl got wind of it through her powerful kink connections and decided to notify each and every person who could have been possibly exposed to it, in spite of the fact that:

- It was someone else's health information.

- It was really none of her damn business since she would not have been exposed as she and the ex were no longer dating at this point.

- She heard about it thirdhand and didn't have all the facts straight. For one, she kept going back and forth over whether it was HSV-1 or HSV-2 when she told people, to this day I don't really know which one.

- Her ex hadn't contracted it himself, and his contact with this girl was fairly light and mostly nonsexual.

To give an understanding of how far this information was spread, I was formally notified because one of my partners had been with another of this guy's exes a few months before we got together. As we compared timelines, we quickly realized that there was no overlap and literally no way that I would have been exposed to this positive result.

The community collectively rolled its eyes, kept (mostly) calm, and carried on. But my buddies and I still reflect sometimes on how stupid the whole thing was. The poor dude eventually recovered from his exiled status. Vigilante Girl has developed a reputation of being a local Chicken Little and nuisance. I don't know what happened to that poor girl who everybody was told was positive. Someone later told me they didn't think the girl even had herpes at all.

It's not sexual safety/STI risk's "fault" per se that sometimes people will use it as a cover for uncomfortable feelings. Sexual safety is important, and so is consent (which is why manipulative people use them, they're sacrosanct in kink/poly circles). However, I think sexual safety is even more pervasive than non-consent as a red herring or bugaboo.

I've seen dozens of instances of people sexually legislating their partners into a kind of mono/poly. Essentially saying "you have to use gloves for hand jobs" and then acting quite a bit more recklessly than how they require others to behave. This isn't just Vigilante Girl. It happens fairly often. And it's an unnerving double standard.

No shame on them for having a good time – it's the hypocrisy that chafes me, not the promiscuity.

The Guardian

And yet... safety is important. I've known polyamorous webs where one person more than any other worried about risk.

These risk-averse individuals serve as protector of the web. A lighthouse who illuminates the water, keeping boats from wrecking on the rocks. A guardian.

Boats and Lighthouses

"I'm going to camp soon, and there are going to be people there I might want to play with. So I wanted to talk about what you're comfortable with," she says.

She tells me who she's interested in, who she's thinking are possibilities. What their deal is. It's a decent amount of detail.

The web has shrunk down significantly as of late, at least on my side of things, so it's an easier conversation than it was six months ago. In a web there's always a person who has the lowest risk tolerance, who has the strictest safety and testing standards. If they're a mature, rational person, I usually lovingly call this member of a web The Guardian. They're like the lighthouse that keeps everyone else from crashing into the rocks.

It's always contextual of course.

And it occurs to me as the two of us talk out over her upcoming trip that we've effectively become the new Guardians. We're Co-Guardians of the web. And together we're setting the terms for unknowns. If there will be leeway. And what that leeway will be.

It's something I haven't seen discussed much in terms of polyamorous relationship systems.

In every web I've ever been in, there are people who gladly welcome these discussions. Who dig easily into the nitty-gritty of risk assessment. Who stay up to date on developments in sexual health. Who can speak about such things in a calm but sensible way.

And there are other people in the web who tend to look at that work and accept its conclusions as reasonable after the fact. Even more rarely, there are folks who question something and add to the strength of the collective risk assessment.

But it all matters. All of it matters to help us get home safely from the adventures we go on.

There are boats and lighthouses, and they all need to find a way to work together. To shed light where it needs to go. Navigate turbulent waters. Stay away from the rocks.

I've absolutely been in a situation where I'm trying to make a decision about sexual health risk and in the moment have stopped and asked myself "What would the Guardian do? Would they be okay with this?"

One magic differentiator between the Guardian and the Secret Sex Police is that the Guardian practices what they preach. They take great pains to safeguard those close to them not just by policing others but through their own personal actions.

And their concerns are rooted in fact, in possible practical outcomes rather than objections raised that secretly cater to unexpressed insecurities.

For more information about sexually transmitted infections and their prevention, please visit www.scarleteen.com

Questions to Ask Yourself

- Do I know my own sexual health status?

- How often do I think it's reasonable to be tested for STIs? For which STIs?

- What are my personal practices for sexual health and safety?

- Are those expectations the same as those I have for my partners and metamours?

Things to Try

- Make sure you're up on your own sexual health knowledge. Our medical understanding is constantly evolving, and new information is being uncovered all the time

- Be clear with others about your expectations surrounding testing.

- Get tested regularly yourself.

- Not only are the first three items on this list just plain old responsible, if it seems like someone else is raising STI objections for some other reason, like hiding their insecurities, you'll be better equipped to talk through the actual facts with them, leaving them with significantly less cover in which to be shady.

ACTIVATOR

STEAMROLLER

Drop what you're doing. We're going on an adventure!

Light

Makes Things Happen

Good at Breaking Ties

Assertive

Dark

Doesn't Always Listen Well

Makes Many Unilateral Decisions

Risks Violating Other's Consent

Steamroller

"I know what we should do," they say.

And before anyone can even chime in, they've pulled out the board game and are passing out the pieces.

"But I was thinking I'd rather –" you start to say.

"I first heard of this game back in college," they continue, loudly speaking over you.

You look around to the others present, and they all look a little uncomfortable.

A little... steamrolled.

But it's harmless enough, so you go along with it. Everyone does.

And you have a good enough time playing this new game. You pick up the rules easily. It's pretty fun.

Until there's a conflict over a play.

"No no no," they say. "You've gotta pay, not me."

"But it says here in the rules that..." you point to the printed instructions.

"Oh no one pays any attention to that. It's obvious that you're new at this," they say. They scoop up your money and tokens, send you back to the start.

Everyone else around you shrugs. It's just a game, so you let it slide. But something makes you worry that next time it won't be a board game you're arguing about.

Ah the steamroller. Of all the metamours I've encountered in my travels, this is one of the most challenging and one that quickly develops a reputation for having loud public fights with people at the slightest sign of conflict. Some may even end up violating sexual consent because they're not open to being told no, let alone taking pains to make sure that they get a yes.

Making matters even worse, the same behaviors that cause problems – steamrolling people and not listening to their input – also prevent them from:

- Realizing that they're doing something that bothers others

- Doing anything about it

This predisposition easily becomes a self-perpetuating cycle in which the steamroller is oblivious to what they're doing and will not only not take measures to improves things but instead double down on their same behavior, even after that behavior is pointed out by multiple people close to them.

Activator

It's not all doom and gloom – some steamrollers do learn from their experiences. Perhaps the consequences of their actions catch up with them. Or enough people approach them over time that it begins to sink in that maybe they should scale it back a little bit.

A steamroller that learns to rein in the behaviors and makes a conscious effort to check in more with those around them can actually be one of the best friends, lovers, or metamours around.

They become a sort of social activator: The person who knows everyone, takes charge of making sure people have a good time. They can easily break ties when there's a gridlock and everyone's shrugging and going "I dunno, where do you want to eat?"

What's key for steamrollers who want to become activators is making sure that they give other people plenty of chance to give their input, saying things like, "This is what I want to do. What do you think?" And being open to dissenting opinions. Or at least civil discussion of them.

A cycle of steamrolling can be a tough to break, particularly if they have a lot of people in their life already who are ill equipped to deal with those behaviors and might even inadvertently be reinforcing them (especially People Pleasers).

Some Steamrollers don't become Activators until they are presented with a rival Steamroller and the two of them are locked in constant conflict. Sometimes this goes terribly – with both parties shifting blame and doubling down on all of their choices. But other times, the two Steamrollers will reach a moment of clarity about themselves and simultaneously both become Activators.

I've found this is especially likely to happen if one or both of them have people in their lives who gently point out that they are prone to a lot of the same aggravating behaviors that their rival is.

Now, this observation is likely to get the Steamroller riled up in the short term, but once they stop carrying on, many of them will reach a point of reckoning which will lead them to more insight about how their behaviors affect other people.

It's not an easy change, but I've known several people who have made this transition, and they're now among some of my favorite people.

A Note About Assertive Communication

When many folks think of assertiveness, they think of sender skills. An assertive person is one who communicates their thoughts and feelings confidently. Openly.

And while this is true, it's not the entire picture. In practice, the most difficult part of assertive communication is the receiver half.

Because an assertive communicator is not only open to speaking their own truths — but also open to hearing and considering those of the person they've talking to. Even when those truths are unpleasant. Or radically different than one's own.

Questions to Ask Yourself

- What's the difference between someone who takes charge in a positive way and someone who does so in a negative way?

- Do you consider yourself an assertive communicator? Why or why not?

- Do you express your thoughts and feelings well, even when you know they might be unpopular?

- Are you open to hearing and honoring the thoughts and feelings of others, even if you don't necessarily agree with them?

- What does that look like?

Things to Try

- Bluntly interrupting. This might feel rude to you, but some steamrollers/activators genuinely don't pick up on subtle social cues and may very well need this.

- When you notice that others around you are also feeling steamrolled, point it out. "Hey, actually a bunch of us would rather do X."

- Model the other half of assertive communication, the receptive half, when you're around them by actively creating opportunities for more shy/introverted people to speak. "Let's see what so-and-so thinks."

CONNECTOR

GOSSIP

Oh my God, you'll never guess what I just heard.

Light

Entertaining to Talk to

Usually Take an Interest in What Other People Are Doing

Can Be Excellent Matchmakers

Dark

Terrible at Keeping Secrets

Make Relationship Transparency Difficult

Oversharing Can Erode Intimacy

Gossip

Everyone knows someone who can't keep a secret. Sometimes it takes a little while to figure out that a new friend is that way, but once we do, we're likely to think twice before letting them know anything we wouldn't want the whole world to know.

But what if the gossip is your metamour?

Many people's definition of emotional intimacy involves the mutual sharing of secrets[19]. So what do you do if your romantic partner is close to someone who is the village gossip?

Do you refrain from sharing things with your partner, worried that they'll tell your metamour, who will share it with everyone they know?

Do you continue to open up to your sweetie, stressing that they are not to tell their other partner what you have told them?

What if they have a rule with your metamour that there is to be complete transparency about what goes in their other relationships? Even if you keep your deepest darkest secrets from your sweetie, are you comfortable with your metamour knowing exactly what's going on in your relationship? And potentially telling everyone they know?

Connectors

And yet, there's something to be said about having a metamour who communicates frequently with others. It can have surprising benefits.

You might think polyamory is wonderful for folks who want to date a lot. And this is true. Predictably, a philosophy that espouses the practice of having simultaneous loving relationships is a good fit for people who want to have them.

But here's the secret:

Poly is even better for folks who enjoy playing matchmaker.

While I've taken my turn as a polysaturated hinge (I once dated five people at the same time), these days I'm a consummate underdater. Many times, I look functionally like I'm in a mono/poly relationship. I spend a lot of time working and writing. And cherish my freedom. Plus, I've been with so many people at this point (I had a wild youth, well before polyamory) that I don't get excited easily. I'm open and loving, sure, but if anything, experience has made me particular.

Even If You Don't Date Much, Polyamory Can Be a Way to Be Surrounded by Love

So why the hell am I still excited about polyamory? Well, setting aside that the possibility of dating people when I want to is a good feeling (and it is), I really enjoy being around people who are in love. Even if it doesn't involve me.

Between my loves, my metamours, my telemours, and my poly friends, I get to watch people be in love. Pretty much constantly. And it's the best.

I suppose it's made more dramatic by the fact that I have lots of poly friends. And by the way, poly friends are arguably the best part of the whole shebang.

The Lost Art of Wingmanship

I frequently serve as a sort of "reference" for friends who are crushing on one another. I'm a great wingman.

"What's her story?" my friend asked me one night at a party as I sat in a hot tub.

"Oh you like her?" I said.

He did. I'd known his crush for years. We chatted about her positive qualities.

I proceeded on a subtle fact-finding mission the next day. "What do you think about him?" I asked her.

"He's fucking adorable," she replied.

"I think you have a shot," I reported back to him.

They've been dating for two years.

And recently, a good friend of mine reported in that they're about to go on a first date with someone they've crushed on for years.

All as a result of my meddling.

Matchmaker, Matchmaker

"Can I place an order?" a friend jokes at a barbecue.

"I make no guarantees," I say. "But what are you looking for?"

Questions to Ask Yourself

- What am I comfortable sharing with my partner, if I knew for sure they would tell my metamour?

- What am I not comfortable sharing?

- Have there been times that I've benefitted from that sort of information being shared?

- Have there been times that I was deeply hurt by it?

Things to Try

- Making expectations clear about what kind of information is shared versus what is not part of your relationship agreement

- Ask your shared partner to keep certain conversations private. If they say they can't, don't tell them.

- Addressing violated expectations surrounding shared information the way you would any other violation of your relationship agreement, within an accountability framework (please see "How to Have an Accountability Talk" on page 141 for more information).

EMPATH

EXPOSED NERVE

If I had a superpower, it would be feeling things deeply.

Light

Attuned to Other's Emotions

Very Perceptive

Usually Quite Tactful

Dark

Extremely Sensitive

May Need Constant Reassurance

Can Lash Out When in Pain

Exposed Nerve

The phone is jumping off the nightstand. Again. I've left it on vibrate because the constant message notification noise was getting on my nerves. Even on silent, it's still somehow managing to make its presence known. Damn buzzing.

`I'm sorry I'm writing so much`, the first text reads.

`Don't be mad at me`, the second one reads.

`It's just that`, says the third.

I put the phone in my bathrobe pocket and walk into the hallway so I don't disturb my bed partner.

"It's just that what?" I say aloud, waiting for the next text.

A few minutes pass, and then it's another flurry of texts. There are a lot of quick fragments and a lot of texts that just say `I'm sorry.` Or `Don't be mad.` But without any context.

And the few short texts I send asking her what she's worried about are lost in the shuffle. She doesn't seem to register or notice them.

So I give up and just wait for another lull in the action. I'm doing my best to piece together what it is she's even saying. She thinks I'm mad at her about something. That she overstepped some kind of boundary...or that I did?

Not sure which.

39 messages and I can't figure it out.

`Hi there`, I write. `I'm not mad at you. I read all of these messages, but I'm not sure what's going on. Did you want to talk about it?`

Her text speed slows down. The content becomes longer and more coherent.

Come to find out, she'd seen me posting on Facebook about something that had nothing to do with her and thought I was mad at her because of it, being passive-aggressive.

I reassure her, explain the real background behind what she saw. What was really going on. And I promise her that if I have any concerns with her that I'll reach out to her and that we'll talk, but that she's been a lovely metamour and that I have nothing but positive regard for her.

Well, except for when she panics like this. It's stressful. And it'd be one thing if this was the only time, but it seems like every time I turn around she's worried because of something I've said. Or because So-and-So liked this other person's post and didn't like hers.

It seems like she's eternally analyzing social situations trying to preempt ever getting hurt and in the process finding no shortage of false alarms.

But I don't say that right now. Because I've only just gotten her calmed down and I'm spent.

For now, I've reassured her again. But as I put up my phone so I can go back to sleep (this time charging it in another room in case she decides to send another frantic series of texts before the night is over, something she's done a few times), it occurs to me that I'm not being completely honest with her. It's going to be a really tough time having that talk, the one about how stressful these late night flurries can be. Since I've seen how upset she can get when I don't even have an issue with her, how is she going to react when I do?

To say that this metamour is very sensitive is putting it lightly. However, when it comes to the Exposed Nerve, a light touch is what's required.

Let's face it: Walking on eggshells makes everything more complicated.

Having certain relationship conversations can be difficult even under ideal circumstances. Throw a person who takes everything personally into the equation, and it can become just that much harder.

According to researcher Elaine Aron[20], 15 to 20 percent of the population is highly sensitive. And despite the stereotypes, it's not just introverts. Dr. Aron found that 30% of highly sensitive people are extroverts!

With sensitivity being so common, odds are good that if you and your partners date enough as polyamorous folks that you'll occasionally have highly sensitive partners or metamours. And you yourself might be highly sensitive yourself.

I have multiple highly sensitive people in my own polyamorous web, and truth be told, as a child I was quick to tears, and I'm kind of a softie.

Empath

We speak of sensitivity as though it's one uniform quality. But it's not. It's an umbrella category that covers a wide range of sensitivities. Some people are simply "sensory defensive"[21] and instead of being emotionally sensitive are overwhelmed by different kinds of stimuli -- textures, noises, lights, crowds, odors, or tastes.

Even when we're speaking strictly of emotional sensitivity, it's not all doom and gloom. In fact, there's a positive flipside to emotional sensitivity.

Some sensitive people not only feel their own feelings deeply, but they are also extremely empathetic and in tune with the emotions of others to an amazing degree. These kinds of sensitive people are sometimes also known as empaths.

Empathy can be a powerful tool for understanding others. While sensitivity can be frustrating in certain context, sensitive people can also be great confidants and wonderful sources of support when you're struggling. The ability to easily pick up and empathize with other people's emotions can be of real benefit to those who themselves need validation and support.

The big downside to being a sensitive person then isn't necessarily the fact that they feel things deeply. It's instead an inability to tolerate negative emotions (both in self and others).

However, this tolerance of negative emotions is actually something can be worked on and strengthened.

Studies[22] have found that the following strategies are helpful to everyone for regulating and reducing negative emotions and that highly sensitive people in particular often benefit from developing them:

- Accepting your feelings

- Not being ashamed of them

- Believing that you can cope just as well as other people can

- Trusting that any negative feelings you have currently will not last forever

- Staying hopeful that you will be able something about your negative feelings eventually

It's difficult for a sensitive person to remember these things, particularly when they're struggling. However, when I've had a particularly close relationship with a metamour, I've found I do have opportunities to remind them of some related principles in a gentle way, as part of the reassurance I provide them:

- There's no should when it comes to emotions. You feel the way you feel.

- There's a difference between acting on a negative emotion and just having one.

- Emotions aren't a sign of weakness.

- You can cry and still be a badass. Actually, depending on what's going on, sometimes crying is the toughest thing you can do.

- Asking for support can be a brave act.

- You got this.

- Feelings don't last forever. Whatever you're feeling right now, it will eventually fade and you'll feel something else.

In addition to these strategies of providing reassurance, I've also developed a personal process of preparing myself to have difficult conversations with sensitive people.

Questions to Ask Yourself

When I go to engage with a sensitive person in what I suspect will be a delicate conversation, I ask myself the following questions:

- Is what I'm going to say constructive? Am I telling them in order to help them and not myself?

- Is this information important to only me? Or will it easily be important to them as well? If not, is there a way that I can share this information that will convey that I value their viewpoint and concerns?

- What possible fears might this conversation stir up in the person I'm talking to? And is there a way I can reassure them preemptively?

Things to Try

- Offering preemptive reassurance

- Being clear that you're not upset with them (even if they don't ask you)

- Being patient if they apologize a lot more than necessary (don't point it out; it usually just makes them more anxious and self-conscious)

Section 4

-

Other

Scenarios

Liar, Liar, Pants on Fire

I don't know anyone who likes to be lied to, but human beings have a tendency to play fast and loose with the truth. According to three studies by researchers Serota, Levin, and Boster, the average person tells 1.65 lies per day[23]. And these were just the ones participants admitted to. With the widespread social stigma surrounding dishonesty, the real figure is likely to be even higher.

But not all lies are created equal. When we speak of "little white lies," we're usually discussing the impact of that lie and the motivation behind it.

People lie for all sorts of reasons, but here are some common ones:

1. To build up their image or make themselves look more important.

2. To save face when they've made a mistake.

3. To avoid consequences.

4. To prevent discord and promote harmony.

5. To solve conflicts.

6. To distract or misdirect from issues they'd rather you not notice.

7. To manipulate people and/or pit them against one another.

8. To protect sensitive information they do not want to disclose or maintain a sense of personal privacy.

9. To hurt the feelings of other people and/or harm their reputations by disseminating false negative information.

10. To practice self-deception, because there are things they don't want to admit to themselves.

11. To feel powerful, like they've tricked someone.

12. As part of a practical joke.

13. To spare someone's feelings (e.g., "What do I think? Oh, you look great in that dress.")

If your metamour lies to you, it can really sting, but like many unfortunate social blunders, not every lie needs to be confronted.

But sometimes, it's imperative.

To sort out the difference, consider the size of the lie, the potential impact of it, the possible motivation behind their dishonesty, and whether there's been a longer, established pattern of dishonest behavior or statements.

Here are some steps for dealing with lies that need to be confronted:

- Document any and all instances of dishonesty. If you have emails or anything written that contradicts what a person is saying, retain those.

- Talk to the person privately about it. Public confrontations are more likely to backfire.

- Don't call them a liar. Address their troubling behavior without expressing judgement about them as a person. Recount what was claimed and that you believe it to be false. Do so directly but gently.

- Give them a chance to explain why they lied. As they explain their reasoning behind the act, carefully examine their body language. Do they appear to still be lying? Or do they appear to be honest in their explanation? If they admit to the lie and apologize, this can be the end of the process. But even then, make sure you talk out the issues involved and end the talk by letting the person know that you really hope it doesn't happen again.

- If the person doesn't admit to the lie and gets defensive instead, bring out any written evidence that proves that they definitely lied to you. Typically at this point, the liar will be quiet or apologize.

- Explain to them that your trust has been damaged by this act of lying.

- Give them another chance to explain why lied. As before, monitor for sincerity and discuss the involved issues thoroughly. Be absolutely certain to stress at the conclusion of the talk that you really don't want it to happen again.

Confronting a liar is actually a specialized kind of accountability talk. Please see "How to Have an Accountability Talk" on page 141 for even more information.

"My Metamour Is Trying to Break Us Up"

Cowboys.

Sadly, there are people out there who assume that a relationship that is open signals trouble in paradise.

Believe it or not, there's a special slang term for people who establish a relationship that starts out polyamorous with the intention of converting it to a monogamous one. This is called being a cowboy (or sometimes cowgirl). The idea is that the cowboy is riding into a herd trying to rope off a filly.

Kind of a fun image but less fun as a reality.

In my personal experiences dating as a polyamorous person as well as working with polyamorous clients as a coach, cowboys are a fairly rare phenomenon. When you do encounter them, they are nearly always people who identify monogamous and are new to dating people in polyamorous relationships. They may openly express that they're okay with dating someone who is involved with others but harbor a secret intent to "turn" the poly person.

It can be rather difficult and hurtful if this would-be cowboy is your metamour.

What should you do if you suspect your metamour is trying to break up your relationship with your partner?

The answer is nothing. Continue to have the best relationship you can have with your partner.

If your partner wants to stay in the relationship with you, they will.

If your relationship really can be broken up by a third party, then it's probably something that should end. True, change is scary, but if they're only marginally committed to you, then you're probably better off. It'll hurt in the short term, but it's saving you time and giving you valuable information.

And if your metamour's attempts fall flat, then you know that your commitment is solid and that it's valuable.

Now, that said, if there are concrete behaviors that your metamour is perpetrating that concern you, you can feel free to share that with your partner – focusing on the observable behaviors themselves and not any spidey sense of impeding doom.

But while they can be frustrating to watch unfold, most potential cowboy situations tend to resolve on their own.

"I Tried to Keep an Open Mind, and It Didn't Work"

So you have an overview of problem behaviors and are equipped with new tools to try out.

That's it, right?

Well, not so fast.

I wish it were so easy to fix all situations. Even though it might come in handy, we can't control what other people do. They always have a choice.

People need to be internally motivated to change. And it's not up to us whether they do.

If changing your perspective on their behavior doesn't help, consider whether or not an accountability talk would be appropriate (please see "How to Have an Accountability Talk" on page 141 for more information on when to tackle one and when not, as well as the process).

Accountability talks can play a vital role in difficult relationships. Sometimes they do the trick – they address the challenging behaviors in question and change things for the better. Other times? It doesn't work out that way. The other person continues to engage in the same behavior. But this outcome is valuable, too, because it shows us how motivated and serious the other person is about changing that behavior. Sometimes they're very motivated but not always.

Sorting out the difference can be helpful because it can bring clarity to the situation. It differentiates a situation that is quite fixable with a little communication and cooperation from the hopeless case (especially after repeated conversations with little to no improvement, or even worsening).

When it comes to working through issues collaboratively, there's no substitute for motivation, good will, and commitment to the process.

Here are some common situations that can be fiendishly difficult – sometimes even impossible – to overcome:

Your Metamour Resents Your Existence

While one would hope that everyone who identifies as polyamorous would be enthusiastic about it, this sadly isn't always the case.

Sometimes an existing relationship will open up where one party is very interested in polyamory and the other reluctantly agrees. Not because they want to be non-monogamous but for a number of less than ideal reasons, including:

- Their partner really wants polyamory, and they want to please their partner.

- They are afraid that they will lose their partner if they don't agree to be polyamorous with them.

- They feel like polyamory is a more enlightened or ethical choice than monogamy.

Or perhaps they're excited about polyamory because of the prospect that they will be allowed to see other people but really do not want their partner to do the same.

And in still other cases, some people who were excited about polyamory in theory find that it is very different in reality and challenges them in ways that they weren't prepared for.

In all of these circumstances, it's very easy for them to view their metamours as an imposition, resenting the fact that they are sharing their partner with someone else, because emotionally they still very much want monogamy.

Sometimes this feeling of resentment is a temporary state as they acclimate to polyamory. After all, most of us were raised in a culture that positions monogamy as the more desirable choice – and indeed often as the only viable way to do relationships long term. So it's understandable, given this, that with this inculturation it can take some time and effort to undo those patterns of thinking.

Meanwhile, their resentment might manifest in a number of different ways: Directly thorny behavior towards metamours, a refusal to meet them, or "pulling rank" by insisting that their partner cancel dates (sometimes as a kind of test to make sure that they're still most important to their sweetie, even with a new partner in the picture).

Extremely frustrating, hurtful behavior that is quite difficult to deal with aside from patience and personal coping.

It can take some time for a person to overcome those behaviors even if they're motivated to change. And if they aren't? Sorry to say, but they are unlikely to change their ways.

Your Metamour Feels Demoted

You've had a good stint at your job. You work at a small company, where they treat you well. Not only do you like your work, but best of all, you're basically an entire department. You have coworkers, sure, but nobody does quite what you do. You're the only one with your job title.

There's no one breathing down your neck while you do your work. And you complete it, managing your workflow just the way you like.

And then one day it all changes. Another person is hired from outside into your department, doing what you do. They're given your same job title, which irks you, because who are they? They just got here. This isn't an entry level position – or is it?

You march into your boss's office and demand a promotion. A raise. A title upgrade.

He stares at you, shocked. You've been doing your work happily all these years, and everything was fine. Why are you raising a fuss now?

Enraged at his response, you throw a stack of papers in his face and walk away.

It's funny how our self-worth can get wrapped up in our relationships.

I've talked to many people over the years who were blindsided by how much going from being their partner's One and Only to being one of multiple people that their partner loves was a hit to their self-esteem. Sadly, this can lead to similar issues as a metamour who resents your existence.

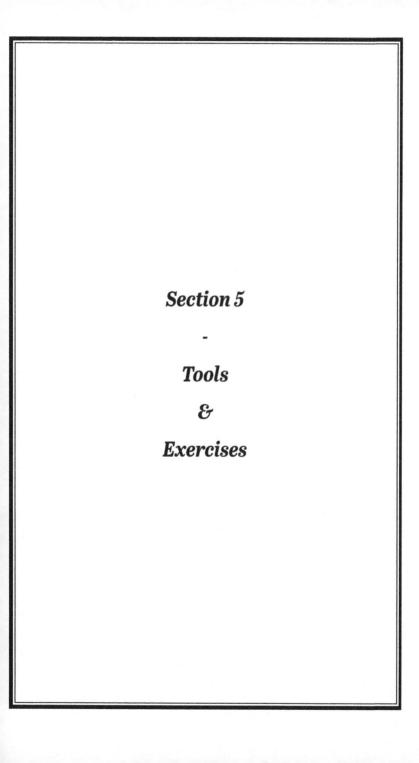

Section 5

-

Tools

&

Exercises

How to Have an Accountability Talk

I've found the framework in Crucial Accountability[24] (by Patterson, Grenny, Maxfield, McMillian, and Switzler, yup 5 authors, it's just that meaty) to be especially helpful.

Because like most things in life, when polyamory is good, it's great. But when it's bad? It's horrid.

Here are 9 steps for having an accountability talk with a partner when things go wrong.

1. Choose What and If

The first step in having an accountability talk is figuring out what the core issue is. What bothers you the most? Especially when we're upset, it's easy to generate a laundry list of concerns.

If a partner doesn't follow your agreed-upon sexual safety rules, you'll likely be upset that they put your health at risk. Or perhaps you're most upset that they broke the promise and violated your trust. Or maybe they lied to you about it after it happened, and that's the core issue.

Dig deep. Sometimes the most important issue isn't the first one you think of.

As much as you may want to address each and every one of these issues in depth with your partner, accountability conversations go better when you have a single issue you're focusing on. It's difficult enough to address violated expectations without the other person becoming defensive, shutting down, and leaving the conversation. If you approach your talk with 12 concerns? Yikes. You're basically guaranteed an unproductive talk. Avoid doing that. Focus on the most important one.

And once you've identified what that issue is, the next step is to identify if you want to have the conversation. If it's a clear-cut case of bad behavior (such as lying and/or breaking a relationship agreement), this could be an easy yes. Especially if there's an established pattern.

In some cases, however, it might be a bit more ambiguous. Returning to the issue of the partner who seems to be ignoring you, there could be good reasons for this. Maybe it's a fluke. An unprecedented level of busyness. And maybe the problem will self-correct.

How do you tell if you should speak up in this circumstance? If you find yourself acting out in other ways or suffering from a nagging conscience, then it might be time to speak up.

2. Master Your Self-Story, Watch Out for the Fundamental Attribution Error

As you approach your partner, you're likely to have all sorts of negative emotions surrounding the violation. So before you open your mouth, get your own head on straight first. You have one shot at opening a new conversation, and first impressions count.

Think through the situation in a way that's as compassionate as possible to your partner. Pretend that you're them. What are some reasons why someone who is a reasonable, rational, decent human being would act that way?

Consider interpersonal, social, or structural obstacles like lack of resources, time, or knowledge. What other people could have influenced them? Do they have the tools to actually keep the commitment? Is there some knowledge gap? A miscommunication?

While we are often rightfully ticked off when people break their promises, it's important to be mindful of the fundamental attribution error[25].

The fundamental attribution error is a cognitive bias that virtually all human beings share in which we tend to explain other people's behavior in terms of their personality and underestimate the role of situational factors affecting them.

So when someone is late to our dinner date, we're more likely to default to thinking of them as disrespectful, irresponsible, or disorganized when in fact there may have been a seven-car pileup on the freeway. Or they were dealing with some emergency (for example, taking a friend to the hospital who had no other way to get there).

3. Describe and Focus on the Gap Between Expectations and Reality

In order to create safety, have the conversation in private and one on one. And get their permission to speak about it. No one likes having a big talk sprung on them when they don't have the time to really address it.

Start the conversation with your partner by plainly and simply describing what you expected to happen and contrasting it with what has happened.

"I expected ABC to happen and XYZ has happened instead."

Do this in as non-blaming a way as possible. Whenever you can, establish common ground. Talk about the values you share. The things you both want.

Avoid drawing harsh conclusions or making personal attacks. Focus on you and your feelings of disappointment surrounding the gap.

Even if you feel the other person has been selfish or reckless, it rarely goes well to tell them that. It's nearly guaranteed to make them defensive. And avoid calling them any names.

You want to discuss the situation and the behavior as the problem, and not them. As soon as they feel like you're defining the problem as them or their character, conversations usually take a turn for the worse.

4. Motivate Through Consequences (Especially Natural Ones)

Once you've described the gap between expectations and reality, explore the consequences of these behaviors. Especially natural ones. Focus on establishing outcomes you both want. And avoiding ones you would both like to never see happen.

What these consequences are will vary depending on the nature of the violation.

But whatever you do, be firm but also be realistic. This isn't about threatening to punish someone. This is about talking about the likely negative effects if this pattern continues.

If this unwanted behavior continuing is likely to lead to your breaking up, it's okay to share that in a level-headed way. But this is not a time to threaten ultimatums that you have no plan of carrying out. If you say that this pattern of behavior is likely to lead to your breaking up, then you had better mean that. (And yes, the most serious violations of trust undoubtedly qualify.)

5. Identify Potential Barriers to Keeping Agreements

Wanting to keep a promise and being able to are in fact two different things. When someone hurts us, it can be easy to confuse them with each other. When speaking with your partner, identify any barriers that might have interfered with their ability to keep the agreement, ones that you came up with in step #2, when you prepared for the conversation by trying to take their perspective.

Giving them the benefit of the doubt where you can goes a long way into actually coming up with ways to correct the behavior. Especially if this is the first violation, or at least the first time you've brought up the issue.

6. Solicit Their Feedback on How to Eliminate Barriers

As you identify potential barriers, solicit their feedback. Ask them why they think these undesirable behaviors happened. What sort of obstacles did they encounter?

You don't need to have the whole problem worked out before approaching them. And being open to their side of the story is an important element of making them feel emotionally safe and part of the problem-solving process (which increases the chances that they will actually follow through).

7. Stay Focused on the Topic at Hand

Of course, as you're discussing the topic at hand, you may find that you get off topic.

Don't allow minor tangents to stray the conversation from the main point.

If a worse issue does emerge and you have to address that, set a reminder regarding the original problem so you can return to it later. And once you've dealt with the emergent issue, return to the original one.

8. Be Firm, Yet Flexible

As you talk through the issues, let your partner know that you don't expect perfection, just their best effort. And part of communicating this meaningfully is remaining flexible.

How can you stay flexible while being firm? The authors of Crucial Accountability advise this statement "If something comes up, let me know as soon as you can." And offer the following example of how this can fit into a larger conversation:

"I want you to live up to your promise. Please don't unilaterally break it…At the same time, I realize that the world can change. Things can come up. Many of these barriers will negate your existing promise. If something does come up, let me know as soon as possible so there are no surprises and so we can decide together how to best handle the situation."

Set up conditions where it's not a simple win/lose. Perfection or atrocious behavior. Give them ways to do better, even if they screw up.

9. Agree on a Plan and Follow Up

And as the final step, agree on a plan to improve the behavior. It could be formal or informal. Many of the best practices for negotiating a relationship agreement apply here as well. Be clear. No tricks. Maybe even write it down.

As part of that plan, it can be helpful to establish check-in times to revisit the discussion. Again, this can be formal or informal depending on the way you both work best and the size of the violation.

For more examples and in-depth instruction on ways to implement accountability, please see "Crucial Accountability: Tools for Resolving Violated Expectations, Broken Commitments, and Bad Behavior".

It was some of the best money I ever personally spent.

Five Steps to Feeling Safe and Secure in Polyamory

Here are five steps to feeling more safe and secure in polyamorous relationships (and in general).

1. Acknowledge Your Feelings

The first step in conquering feelings of insecurity is acknowledging them. This is because getting rid of those feelings isn't the same as pretending you don't feel them in the first place. In fact, when people start to feel insecure, they often become ashamed of the insecurity, which starts a secondary trauma loop, where they're beating themselves up over and over again, punishing themselves for feeling (pretty normal) negative feelings. And beating yourself up and shaming yourself works against feeling secure.

Shame is the real killer. Not fear, anxiety, jealousy, insecurity. But shame. In basic survival terms, if the tribe rejects you, you die. Exile was death to our ancestors. Shame is a sense that you are unacceptable, that you don't belong. And your brain feels like it's life or death.

The worst part is that feeling bad about feeling bad? It's especially true for really good people.

Because it's not the feeling itself but our shame about the feeling – just like it's never the mistake that gets you, it's the cover-up.

While you can cover up those unacceptable feelings, by not sharing them, there's one person you'll never hide them from: Yourself. So avoid covering up your feelings and make sure you acknowledge them.

2. But Don't Jump to Conclusions!

> "You cannot make yourself feel something you do not feel, but you can make yourself do right in spite of your feelings."

-Pearl Buck

However, acknowledging feelings of insecurity isn't the same thing as trusting your emotions completely. Or saying that our fears are going to come true.

Our emotional systems have evolved to make snap judgments. To quickly identify threats and differentiate predator from prey. For that purpose, fear responses are perfectly well suited. But what protects us in the wild from getting eaten? Well, it doesn't work so well for modern relationships, which are less life and death and much more full of nuance.

So even though you might feel worried, don't assume that your world is actually ending. And just because you feel bad, it also doesn't mean that anybody did anything wrong (though it could).

Rather than lashing out or doing something you regret, take a second to breathe and dig a little deeper into those feelings.

3. When You Feel Bad About Something, Ask Yourself "Why?"

Let's say you felt bad when you saw your partner flirting with another person. Why is that? What is that feeling telling you?

It can be uncomfortable to sit in this place, but do it as much as you can. Follow your fear to its logical conclusion.

Are you worried about getting replaced? Abandoned?

Part of what makes fear so powerful is that it's irrational and thrives in secrecy. And it's by dragging fear's arguments into the light of day and forcing fear to defend itself that we start to rob it of its power.

Sometimes, our fears are justified. Every now and then, there is a logical, well-founded basis to our fear. However, the vast majority of the time, fear overstates its case. Besides, in cases where our fears are justified, it's better to be in touch with that and act according to that reality.

It's as Carl Sagan once said: "It is far better to grasp the universe as it really is than to persist in delusion, however satisfying and reassuring."

4. Identify and Question the Underlying Assumptions

Once you know what your fear is telling you, look for any underlying assumptions that it's making.

Folks who are new to polyamory frequently worry about a new partner outperforming them sexually. The underlying assumption here is that people select partners solely based on their sexual prowess. In situations like these, I've found it helpful to ask myself: What are other reasons that a partner could find value from being with me? What are some signs that my relationship is actually going well?

I also find it helpful to compare my assumptions about others to how I actually feel, think, and act. I struggled for a long time with the idea that sex was some sort of competition with runners-up facing the risk of being replaced — until I realized that's not how I view or treat people. And because it's not a view that I support or respect very much, I realized that if someone does view or treat people this way, they're fundamentally incompatible with me. Therefore, someone who would replace me in this way is someone I don't actually want to be with.

Depending on your specific concerns, the exact process and how you work through it will be different. What's important is thinking through your reactions and testing them against reality.

5. Remember: When It Comes to Feeling Secure, the Secret Ingredient Is Time

I think we've all been there. Sitting there, struggling over a particularly difficult problem. Pulling out our hair. Asking ourselves What the HELL are we going to do about this?

It feels like we're making absolutely no progress. Frustrated, we stop what we're doing and take a break. Do something else, even goof off for a while.

And after a bit of time away, we revisit the problem…and immediately feel stupid. Of COURSE. It was so OBVIOUS. How did we not see this the first time?

This phenomenon, getting past a mental block when we revisit a problem after taking a break from it? It's well documented in psychology.

It's called incubation effect.

For me, building up my sense of personal security followed this kind of timeline. I agonized. Practiced and practiced. And felt like I was making no progress. And then one day? I made a ton. Out of the blue. Kind of like the loading bar on your computer that sits at 10% for hours and then zips up the last 90% while you're looking away for two seconds.

So don't despair if you don't feel secure overnight. Keep digging. Keep analyzing. And keep on braving uncertainty. The only way past the discomfort is through it.

As Pamela Madsen writes in Shameless[26]:

> I don't think that staying with discomfort comes naturally. And finding ways to be with your discomfort is an essential skill for staying in the race. Any personal growth usually involves some kind of ability to stay with feelings of discomfort.
>
> Let's face it. If you are a seeker of any kind you will push boundaries. When we reach for personal transformation and start pushing edges and boundaries in our lives — we meet "the big work" and feelings of discomfort and wanting to flee from change surface.

Challenge the Underlying Assumptions of Toxic Monogamy

You're not alone, transitioning from a monogamous way of thinking to a polyamorous one. It can be quite an adjustment.

You might blame yourself for this difficulty. Or you might blame polyamory. In reality, it's neither of these things.

The problem lies with toxic monogamy culture.

What is toxic monogamy culture? It's a set of societal beliefs that teach us that monogamy is the only ethical and healthy way to do relationships. And it does so in a way that's not only damaging to non-monogamy but to having healthy relationships of any sort, whether they're monogamous or polyamorous. Toxic monogamy is basically the worst.

To be clear: Not all monogamy is toxic, and not all aspects of monogamy are toxic.

Monogamy in and of itself has so many good qualities. Sexual exclusivity in particular has a large upside. When practiced perfectly (although not always the case, even when it's meant to be), monogamy carries a lower STI risk. Though I've been polyamorous for quite some time, I could easily be sexually monogamous, if I could still have emotional connections with more than one person.

However, many people in long-term monogamous relationships become emotionally and socially isolated in a profound way. This is because a number of socially connected behaviors are perceived as infidelities. Toxic monogamy culturally trains us to be on high alert to detect cheating in our own relationships and the ones of those around us. This makes us overly sensitive to prosocial acts that could signal something insidious lurking beneath the surface.

For example, I recall a conversation I overheard between people who agreed that posting pictures with members of the opposite sex on Facebook was in fact cheating on your significant other. Even setting aside the fact that I'm not straight, this idea perplexed me.

As Noah Brand writes[27]:

> Hegemonic heterosexuality is the model for straight relationships that carries as many damaging, ridiculous, impossible assumptions and requirements as does hegemonic masculinity. Shall we list a few?
>
> Relationships are about finding The One you'll spend the rest of your life with. Naturally, a jealous and possessive form of monogamy is a strict requirement. It is necessary to hate all of one's exes, because they were not The One, and one must also be jealous of all one's partner's exes, because they touched your property before you even got there.

Given all this, it's not that adjusting to polyamory is impossible. Rather, it's that when left unchecked and unchallenged that the beliefs that accompany toxic monogamy will consistently torture a person in a polyamorous environment.

To combat this, challenge the underlying assumptions of toxic monogamy:

- Affection is zero sum. When you care for someone, that leaves less caring to give to others.

- One person must meet every possible emotional and social need that we have.

- We must do whatever is needed to protect The Relationship — a simultaneously fragile and all-important entity. If this involves complete isolation, then so be it.

- If a love is true and valid, we will never, ever be attracted to anyone else. Ever.

- If the intensity of that love changes, there is something wrong.

- If we are attracted to someone else, this means that our love isn't true. Or we're a horrible person. Or both. Probably both.

Even long-time polyamorous folks can struggle with some of this. These beliefs linger as nagging doubts. Even though we have actively rejected monogamy as a relationship style, we were raised in the same world. Toxic monogamy was modeled for us over and over again (through media, the relationships of others, etc.).

But it's important to realize that affection isn't zero sum. We don't care less for one person because we care for another. It sounds absurd to suggest that people who have more children love each child less than those who have fewer, but somehow when we say this of romantic love, a lot of people believe it.

I'll tell you, as a person with experience of being in multiple loving relationships at once, it just doesn't work that way: You can absolutely love more than one person at a time. Deeply. And differently.

Whether you're polyamorous, monogamous, or somewhere in between, one thing is true: Toxic monogamy is terrible for you.

Counter to what one might think, acting as though love is scarce is an easy way to lose it. Worrying you'll lose someone can drive them away. At the very least it can drive a wedge between you.

A Readers' Discussion Guide for Vees

Look in the Mirror First

Try to think of at least three times that you were someone else's difficult person. Try to remember why you chose to behave the way you did. What was going through your mind at the time?

How could you have chosen to behave a little differently? Why didn't you?

There are really no right or wrong answers here. Sometimes we're doing the best we can and are still someone else's difficult person. Other times we might have acted differently had we thought about things from a different perspective, knew what had happened next, etc.

Discuss what you have written with your metamour and shared partner.

Meeting Your Metamours or Not

How do you feel about meeting metamours? Do you feel like it's essential or optional? What are some reasons you can think of that you might not want to meet your metamours?

If you've been polyamorous for a while, has this view changed over that time or stayed the same? If it's changed, what experiences informed that change?

General Principles of Dealing with Difficult People

Think back on times that you had to deal with difficult people outside of polyamory. This could involve interactions with family members, coworkers, and mutual friends. Can you remember times that went very well? How about ones that didn't go so well? Is there anything you learned that you could possibly apply to your polyamorous relationships?

Identify What's Bothering You and Why

Think of someone you struggle to get along with or have in the past. It could be your current metamour, a past one, or someone else entirely.

Try asking yourself the following questions:

1. "Why don't I like this person?" or if you like them well enough but are still experiencing stress, "What is really bothering me about them?

2. Do I feel like they're smarter, funnier, prettier, sexier, or somehow "better" than me?

3. Do they remind me of someone from my past that I don't like?

4. Do they have a reputation for treating others badly?

Additional questions to ask if this person is a past or present metamour:

5. Do I feel like this partner is too different from me? And that it means that my partner doesn't really want someone like me?

6. Did they treat my partner badly in the past?

7. Are they treating my partner badly now or doing something else that's causing problems?

Spend some time really thinking about these questions. Dig as deeply as you can. There might be multiple reasons.

Once you're done writing these thoughts down, you might be comfortable sharing these observations with the rest of your vee, and you might want to keep them to yourself.

The important thing is to really devote thought to them.

Empathy: Try to Understand Them

Four empathy-building exercises are described in this section:

- Make Opportunities to Listen

- Reverse Engineer

- The Shape-Shifting Game

- Metta-mours: The Loving-Kindness Meditation

Of these exercises, which appeals to you the most? Which appeals to you the least? Why?

Pick two of these to start doing. Practice them for a week.

At the end of the week, meet up with the other two-thirds of your vee to discuss the experience. Did you feel a change? Did you feel silly? Was it fun? What did you learn about yourself (and possibly others)?

Boundaries

Write down five basic boundaries that are important to you in relationships.

Share these with the other members of your vee. Which ones do you share? Which ones are unique to you?

After speaking with your partner and metamour, are there some they've listed that you feel are important as well?

Bucket 1: Things You Can Control

Bucket 2: Things You Can Influence

Bucket 3: Things Over Which You Have Absolutely No Control

Consider the following scenarios and sort them into the appropriate bucket, explaining why:

Scenario #1:

You've made plans to see your sweetie, but their workplace calls them last minute asking if they can come in and cover a shift.

Scenario #2:

Your sweetie looks like they want to see someone new, but you're worried that they will overextend themselves. You have difficulty getting enough time with them as it is, and you're far from the only obligation in their life.

Scenario #3:

Your new metamour requires full transparency about all of their partners' other relationships. This goes beyond simply knowing who their partner is seeing and involves requiring to know many intimate details.

Scenario #4:

You have a habit of being extremely late to all of your appointments. It seems to plague you pretty consistently. It's not only annoying to those around you but even causes logistical problems occasionally.

Scenario #5:

Your partner often returns home late from dates, causing you frequent worry, especially when those dates are late at night.

Compare your answers with those of the other people in your vee. Do you all put things in the same buckets? If there are differences, what are they and why?

Can any of these conflicts be resolved by setting first-degree boundaries? Why or why not?

A Crash Course in Mindfulness

Five mindfulness exercises are described in this section:

- Pay close attention to something you do on a daily, or more than daily, basis.

- Deep breathing.

- Grounded sitting.

- Focus on sounds.

- Emotional check-in.

Over the next five days, pick a new one of these to do through-out the day. Once you've tried them all for at least one day, check back in with the rest of your vee.

Discuss how the experience went. Did anything surprise you? Do you feel any different?

Did you have one that was your favorite? One that you really didn't like? Why?

The Ladder of Inference

Think of a time where you climbed the ladder of inference in a way that was really unhelpful. Ask yourself the following:

- How did you jump to conclusions?

- What steps did you miss in your thinking?

- What facts didn't you consider?

- What assumptions did you make? Were those assumptions reality based?

- What beliefs guided you through your decision-making process? Were those beliefs well founded? Why or why not?

- What did you decide you focus on? What did you ignore?

- What were the consequences of skipping up the rungs on the ladder of inference?

- Are there are any lessons that you can bring into future decision-making?

Be Kind to Yourself

Think of the last time you made a mistake. What was it? How did you feel about yourself? How did you react? Did you beat yourself up for it, finding it difficult to get over the fact that you made the mistake, or did you let it go easily?

Think about a close friend. What if they made that same mistake? How would you feel about them? Would you continue to judge them and find it difficult to get over, or would you find it fairly easy to let them off the hook?

If your most recent mistake was a small one, think of a larger mistake and ask yourself the same questions (about both yourself and a close friend). If your most recent mistake was a large one, ask the same questions about a small one.

Compare your reaction to small mistakes (made by self and others) to your reaction for large mistakes. Are they similar? Do they differ?

If the reactions differ between small and large mistakes, why do you think that is?

If your reactions to mistakes that you make versus ones that a close friend would make differ, why do you think that is?

Light and Shadow, a Note About Metamour Types

It is a rare person who doesn't have some kind of positive quality. Looking back through my own life, I can't think of a person. Even the most difficult people, ones who engaged in harmful or abusive behaviors, had positive attributes.

For this exercise, think of your least favorite people.

What are some of their positive qualities?

What are some of the upsides of the behaviors that you find negative? (Maybe it was damaging in one context, and that ruined the relationship for you, but you can see other ways that it benefited them or others, even if the negative outweighed the positive).

Depending on the person and their behaviors, this might not be an easy exercise but really try.

People Pleaser / Caretaker

Do you feel like you have the qualities of a people pleaser or caretaker?

If yes, in what ways do you think this can be a strength? In what ways can it cause problems for you or those around you?

Do you feel like you've had a past or present metamour who was a people pleaser or caretaker?

If yes, in what ways do you think this can be a strength? In what ways can it cause problems for you or others?

Do you feel like you operate under more of an Ask Culture paradigm, a Guess Culture paradigm, or somewhere in between? How about your metamour or shared partner? Are you similar or different?

If different, how do those differences play out? Can you think of times when knowing about the difference between Ask and Guess Culture could have been helpful?

Buttinski / #1 Metamour

Do you feel a lot of compersion for your partner's other relationships?

How do you feel about the need for privacy in polyamorous relationships? How do you feel about the need for transparency in polyamorous relationships?

If you feel like both are important, how have you found balance between the two?

How do you feel about metamours in general? Is getting a new metamour exciting to you? Or is it something that's more of a negative global feeling? Or are you neutral? Or does it really depend on the person?

Blame-Shifting Ninja / Accountability Expert

Think back on situations where your skills came into question. Do you have more of a fixed mindset or a growth mindset?

Some people find that their opinion of this changes over time. That's okay. If your opinion has changed, when did that change and why?

Think of a time where someone blamed you for something in a way that made it hard for you to talk things over and solve the problem. How could that conversation have gone differently and been more productive? What would an accountability talk look like in that same situation?

Think of a time where you were quick to blame someone else. Consider the same questions: How could that conversation have gone differently and been more productive? What would an accountability talk look like in that same situation?

Drama Llama / Life of the Party

Consider the five conflict styles: Accommodating, Avoiding, Collaborating, Competing, Compromising.

Think about how you have addressed conflicts in the past.

Do you have a default style? Which style do you use the least?

Can you think of some situations where you used one style and some situations where you used another? What were the outcomes? How did it go?

Consider the alternative styles in those same scenarios. How might have the outcome been different?

Control Freak / Organizer

Of the 24 potentially controlling behaviors listed at the beginning of this chapter, how many have you experienced people doing to you?

Now flip it around. Looking at this same list, how many of these behaviors have you done to others? Are there some that you used to do but you don't do anymore? Are there ones that you currently do that perhaps you would like to do less frequently?

Think of all the people you know. Who would you say is most organized – or, if you prefer, who is the "adultiest adult?"

Why do you say that? What qualities do they possess? What behaviors do they perform?

Rule Breaker / Daredevil

Consider the following questions:

What are the consequences for violating the relationship agreements that apply to me?

Could I forgive someone for violating our relationship agreement? If so, what factors would influence my ability to forgive and forget – or at least work with them to do better?

Secret Sex Police / Guardian

Ask yourself the following questions:

Do I understand the expectations in my relationship regarding safer sex practices?

Am I clear not only on what is expected of me but why?

Do we have a procedure for if someone gets a positive STI result (for me, a partner, or metamour)? If so, what is that procedure?

Steamroller / Activator

Do you consider yourself an assertive communicator? Why or why not?

Do you express your thoughts and feelings well, even when you know they might be unpopular?

Are you open to hearing and honoring the thoughts and feelings of others, even if you don't necessarily agree with them?

Do you give people a chance to give their input? E.g., asking "This is what I want to do. What do you think?"

If the answer to this final question is no, experiment with doing so. See what happens.

Exposed Nerve/Empath

Think of a time when you were really upset and ask yourself the following questions:

How did it feel?

How long did it last?

What kind of support could you have used when you were going through that?

Think about other times that you were upset. Ask yourself the same questions. Considering all of the events in order, do you feel like over time you're dealing with negative feelings better, worse, or about the same?

Appendix

Glossary

Accountability Mindset

A way of dealing with mistakes where the focus is on keeping agreements and being respectful to one another. An accountability framework assumes that everyone is capable of making mistakes or falling short of commitments and focuses on ways to prevent unfortunate things from happening in the future. Its opposite is a blame mindset.

Ask Culture

The expectation that it's OK to ask for anything at all, but you realize and accept that you might get no for an answer.

Blame Mindset

A way of dealing with mistakes where our highest priority is to make sure that mistake reflects on the other person and not us. Its opposite is an accountability mindset.

Buttinski Sign

A slang term for instances when someone exercises poor boundaries and "butts in" inappropriately in their partner's other relationship

Compersion

A state of sympathetic joy in which a person is happy because of another person's happiness (even if it has little or no direct benefit to them). Sometimes called "the opposite of jealousy." Also known as confelicity or mudita (from Pali and Sanskrit).

Cowboy/Cowgirl

A person who establishes a relationship that starts out polyamorous with the intention of converting it to a monogamous one. The idea is that they are riding into a herd trying to rope off a filly.

Descriptive Hierarchy

A style of hierarchical polyamory in which certain relationships are considered higher priority than others but only for the time being. In a descriptive hierarchy, future dynamics are not dictated. Labels used are only describing the current state of the hierarchy, usually based on things like level of entanglement, length of relationships, etc.

Double Bind

When a person sends out two different messages, both of which conflicts with the other. This causes situations where no matter what you're doing, you're going to do "the wrong thing" and be criticized. A double bind is also known as "being between a rock and a hard place" and "damned if you do, damned if you don't."

Dyad

Another term for couple, or a pair of romantic partners

Fixed Mindset

A belief that people are born with a natural ability level and that these are fixed traits. People with this mindset believe they have a certain amount of ability. For example, rather than making concerted efforts to improve their personal education, a person with a fixed mindset regarding intelligence would develop the goal to appear smart and to never, ever look dumb. The opposite of this mindset is a growth mindset.

Fluid Bond

A term commonly used in polyamorous circles to describe an arrangement between people where they have sex without a condom or some other barrier (dental dam, etc.)

Fundamental Attribution Error

A cognitive bias that virtually all human beings share in which we tend to explain other people's behavior in terms of their personality and underestimate the role of situational factors affecting them

Growth Mindset

A belief that people can develop their talents and skills through concerted effort. The opposite of this mindset is a fixed mindset.

Guess Culture

The expectation that you should avoid putting a request into words unless you're pretty sure the answer will be yes.

Hierarchical Polyamory

A style of polyamory in which certain relationships are considered higher priority than others. This is usually noted by calling some relationships "primary" and others "secondary." Can take the form of descriptive or prescriptive hierarchy.

Hinge

A person having relationships with two (or more) partners who aren't romantically involved with one another

Incubation Effect

Our tendency to get past a mental block when we revisit a problem after taking a break from it

Kitchen Table Polyamory

A style of polyamory where everyone in the polyamorous relationship system is comfortable sitting down at the kitchen table with one another to have a cup of coffee (or hot chocolate, soda, whatever is your speed)

Ladder of Inference

> A process we go through whenever we think without realizing we do, starting with facts but attaching inference and the meanings we draw from other people's actions in order to form our conclusions and decide how to act

Metamour

> A partner's other partner

Mindfulness

> The state of being aware of something without wishing it were different, a focused awareness on the present moment and acceptance of one's thoughts, feelings, and physical sensations

New Relationship Energy (a.k.a. NRE)

> A mental and emotional state experienced at the beginning of romantic and sexual relationships. Also known as limerence.

Non-Hierarchical Polyamory

> A style of polyamory in which no relationship is ranked or put before the other. There are no primaries or secondaries (or tertiaries).

Old Relationship Energy (a.k.a. ORE)

> The dynamic of a long-standing established romantic or sexual relationship. Related to the Greek concept of pragma or mature love. Also known as companionate love.

Open Polyamory

A style of polyamory in which relationships are open to new partners

Parallel Polyamory

A style of polyamory where relationships run in parallel and metamours don't meet or interact with one another

Polyfidelity

A style of polyamory in which multiple people are committed to one another and are not open to new partners

Polyamory

The practice of participating simultaneously in more than one serious romantic or sexual relationship with the knowledge and consent of all partners

Polysaturated

A state in which a polyamorous person is dating enough people that they couldn't manage more relationships even if they wanted to

Prescriptive Hierarchy

A style of hierarchical polyamory in which certain relationships are designated higher priority than others with the understanding that they always will be

Primary Relationship

A relationship that is prioritized over others and/or one that involves significant entanglement, e.g., living together, sharing finances, raising children, seeing each other frequently, etc. Other terms that are commonly used include anchor partner or nesting partner. Note: Polyamorous people can have multiple primary relationships.

Relationship Escalator

A widely held cultural belief about relationships that they must follow a particular pattern, leading to progressively more serious commitment

Secondary Relationship

A relationship that is considered generally lower priority than a primary relationship and/or one that is lower entanglement

Self-Compassion

The act of extending compassion to yourself, especially in circumstances where you feel like you've made a mistake or failed

Sexile

A portmanteau for "sexual exile." When one partner stays out of the shared dwelling when they know their partner has a date at the house, in order to give them some privacy.

Solo Polyamory (a.k.a. solo poly)

A category of polyamory that covers a wide range of relationships that take a "free agent" approach to poly. Many solo polyamorists don't choose to share a home or finances with intimate partners generally tend to emphasize themselves as individuals and not part of a couple or triad.

Square

A relationship system that refers to four people, most commonly two couples (but not always)

Telemour

Your metamour's other partner

Tertiary Relationship

A relationship where partners see each other infrequently. Very low entanglement. These are also sometimes known as comet relationships.

Throuple

A three-person couple. See also: Triad

Toxic Monogamy Culture

A set of societal beliefs that teach that monogamy is the only ethical and healthy way to do relationships and does so in a way that's not only damaging to non-monogamy but to having healthy relationships of any sort, whether they're monogamous or polyamorous

Transference

Unconsciously projecting feelings we have for a person we've known previously onto a new person

Triad

A group of three people who are all romantically involved with one another in some way (less commonly also known as a throuple)

Triangular Communication

Communication where people do not directly speak with one another but instead rely on a third party to convey messages between them

Unicorn

Polyamorous, bisexual person (especially a woman) who will date both members of a couple

Unicorn Hunter

A couple (especially a heterosexual one) who opens up their relationship looking to date a unicorn together

Vee

A type of relationship involving three people in which two of the members share a partner in common but aren't involved with one another. Gets its name from the letter V. The shared partner is commonly called a hinge.

Veto Power

The ability to unilaterally end the relationship your partner is having with someone else

Citations

1. Senge, P. M. (2006). The fifth discipline: the art and practice of the learning organization. London: Currency Doubleday.

2. Owad, T. (2006, January 4). Confirmation bias: A ubiquitous phenomenon in many guises. Review of General Psychology 2(2), 175-220.

3. Self-Compassion Exercises by Dr. Kristin Neff. (n.d.). Retrieved September 21, 2017, from http://self-compassion. org/category/exercises/

4. Breines, J. G., & Chen, S. (n.d.). Self-compassion increases self-improvement motivation. PsycEXTRA Dataset. doi:10.1037/e512142015-364

5. Baumeister, R., Campbell, J., Krueger, J., & Volis, K. (2003). Does high self-esteem cause better performance, interpersonal success, happiness and healthier lifestyles?Psychological science in the public interest, 4, 1 – 44.

6. Twenge, J. M., & Campbell, W. K. (2010). The narcissism epidemic: living in the age of entitlement. New York: Free Press.

7. Eichler, A. (2010, May 12). Askers vs. guessers. Retrieved September 20, 2017, from https://www.theatlantic.com/ national/archive/2010/05/askers-vs-guessers/340891/

8. What's the middle ground between 'F.U!' and 'Welcome!'? (n.d.). Retrieved September 20, 2017, from http://ask.metafil-ter.com/55153/Whats-the-middle-ground-between-FU-and-Welcome#830421

9. Dweck, C. S. (2012). Mindset: Changing the way you think to fulfil your potential. London: Little Brown Book Company.

10. Drama. (n.d.). Retrieved October 05, 2017, from https://www.merriam-webster.com/dictionary/drama

11. Lucado, M. (2011). When God whispers your name. Nashville, TN: Thomas Nelson.

12. Kilmann, R. H., & Thomas, K. W. (1977). Developing a Forced-Choice Measure of Conflict-Handling Behavior: The "Mode" Instrument. Educational and Psychological Measurement, 37(2), 309-325. doi:10.1177/001316447703700204

13. E.g., Loftus, E. F., & Palmer, J. C. (1974). Reconstruction of auto-mobile destruction: An example of the interaction between language and memory. Journal of Verbal Learning and Verbal Behavior, 13, 585-589; Yuille, J. C., & Cutshall, J. L. (1986). A case study of eyewitness memory of a crime. Journal of Applied Psychology, 71(2), 291, etc

14. Cottrell, N. B., Wack, D. L., Sekerak, G. J., & Rittle, R. H. (1968). Social facilitation of dominant responses by the presence of an audience and the mere presence of others. Journal of personality and social psychology, 9(3), 245.

15. Gilbert, P., Mcewan, K., Bellew, R., Mills, A., & Gale, C. (2009). The dark side of competition: How competitive behaviour and striving to avoid inferiority are linked to depression, anxiety, stress and self-harm. Psychology and Psychotherapy: Theory, Research and Practice, 82(2), 123-136. doi:10.1348/147608308x379806

16. Numeroff, L. J., & Bond, F. (1985). If you give a mouse a cookie. (Reading Rainbow, 97.). New York: Harper.

17. Siebert, A., Pintarich, K., & Siebert, M. (2010). The survivor personality: why some people are stronger, smarter, and more skillful at handling lifes difficulties-- and how you can be, too. New York: Perigree.

18. 'Adult' as a Verb. (n.d.). Retrieved October 03, 2017, from https://www.merriam-webster.com/words-at-play/adulting

19. Laurencaeu, Jean-Philippe; Lisa Feldman Barrett; Michael J. Rovine (2005). "The interpersonal process model of intimacy in marriage: a daily diary and multilevel modeling approach". Journal of Family Psychology. 19 (2): 314–323. doi:10.1037/0893-3200.19.2.314.

20. Aron, E. (1997). The highly sensitive person: How to thrive when the world overwhelms you. New York: Broadway Books.

21. Heller, S. (2003). Too loud, too bright, too fast, too tight: What to do if you are sensory defensive in an overstimulating world. New York: Quill.

22. Brindle, K., Moulding, R., Bakker, K., & Nedeljkovic, M. (2015). Is the relationship between sensory-processing sensitivity and negative affect mediated by emotional regulation? Australian Journal of Psychology,67(4), 214-221. doi:10.1111/ajpy.12084

23. Serota, K. B., Levine, T. R., & Boster, F. J. (2010). The Prevalence of Lying in America: Three Studies of Self-Reported Lies. Human Communication Research, 36(1), 2-25. doi:10.1111/j.1468-2958.2009.01366.x

24. Patterson, K. (2013). Crucial accountability: tools for resolving violated expectations, broken commitments, and bad behavior. New York: McGraw-Hill.

25. Jones, E. E., & Harris, V. A. (1967). The attribution of attitudes. Journal of Experimental Social Psychology, 3(1), 1-24. doi:10.1016/0022-1031(67)90034-0

26. Madsen, P. (2011). Shameless: How I ditched the diet, got naked, found true pleasure…and somehow got home in time to cook dinner. Emmaus, PA: Rodale.

27. Brand, N. (2012, March 13). Hegemonic heterosexuality. Retrieved March 21, 2017, from https://goodmenproject. com/sex-relationships/hegemonic-heterosexuality/

About the Author

Page Turner

Page Turner is the editor-in-chief of the popular website Poly Land, as well as the award-winning author of three books. She's been cited as a relationship expert in a variety of media publications including The Huffington Post, Glamour, Self, and Bustle. She tries to be the best metamour that she can possibly be.

Also by Page Turner

Poly Land: My Brutally Honest Adventures in Polyamory

A Geek's Guide to Unicorn Ranching: Advice for Couples Seeking Another Partner

Visit her on the web at https://poly.land

Made in the USA
Monee, IL
28 January 2023

26534743R00121